Twayne's English Authors Series

Sylvia E. Bowman, *Editor*

INDIANA UNIVERSITY

Graham Greene

 3

Graham Greene

By A. A. De VITIS

Purdue University

Twayne Publishers, Inc.   ::   New York

Preface

"It is only the infinite mercy and love of God that has prevented us from tearing ourselves to pieces and destroying His entire creation long ago," says Thomas Merton in *The Seven Storey Mountain.* And he then states: "People seem to think that it is in some way a proof that no merciful God exists, if we have so many wars. On the contrary, consider how in spite of centuries of sin and greed and lust and cruelty and hatred and avarice and oppression and injustice, spawned and bred by the free wills of men, the human race can still recover, each time, and can still produce men and women who overcome evil with good, hatred with love, greed with charity, lust and cruelty with sanctity." [1] Compare Bertrand Russell who writes in *The Impact of Science on Society:*

There are certain things that our age needs, and certain things that it should avoid. It needs compassion and a wish that mankind should be happy; it needs the desire for knowledge and the determination to eschew pleasant myths; it needs, above all, courageous hope and the impulse to creativeness. The things that it must avoid, and that have brought it to the brink of catastrophe, are cruelty, envy, greed, competitiveness, search for irrational subjective certainty, and what Freudians call the death wish.

The root of the matter is a very simple and old-fashioned thing, a thing so simple that I am almost ashamed to mention it, for fear of the derisive smile with which wise cynics will greet my words. The thing I mean—please forgive me for mentioning it—is love, Christian love, or compassion. If you feel this, you have a motive for existence, a guide in action, a reason for courage, an imperative necessity for intellectual honesty. If you feel this, you have all that anybody should feel in the way of religion. Although you may not find happiness, you will never know the deep despair of those whose life is aimless and void of purpose; for there is always something that you can do to diminish the awful sum of human misery. [2]

Although Merton would disagree with Russell's statement concerning the place of formal religion in everyday life, he would accept the spirit in which it was written; for, mutually, they advocate love and compassion, and oppose them to hate.

In this book I have endeavored to explain what use Graham Greene makes of religious subject matter and religious belief. Since the religious idea informs much of his work, I have, by analyzing the place of religion in the overall pattern of his novels, traced—as far as possible—the development of his thought and of his art.

In recent years many important writers have become preoccupied with religious themes. Wherever possible I have drawn parallels and pointed out similarities. André Gide from his *Pastoral Symphony* to *The Counterfeiters* shows a penetrating awareness of the place of religion in contemporary life. His *Journals* may be opened at almost any point to reveal how the "arch heretic"—as Mauriac and Maritain consider Gide—fought a personal battle with God that was reflected in his novels. This conflict is revealed in all its aspects in Gide's correspondence with Paul Claudel, himself one of the most important of the writers in France who made use of religious subject matter. Claudel's dramas are strange and enchanting: in *Tidings Brought to Mary,* for example, he makes use of a "virgin" birth to test the faith of a medieval community. François Mauriac, in my opinion the most brilliant of contemporary novelists, follows the teachings of his Church and creates some of the most penetrating studies of hypocrisy, greed, and lust ever written. His influence on the work of Graham Greene is discussed later on. Georges Bernanos and, earlier, Léon Bloy, as well as Claudel and Mauriac, write within a frame of reference that is specifically Catholic; they are widely read, challenging comparison with their English contemporaries. In the United States William Faulkner, in a nebulous manner, parallels the European interest in the Christian myth. *Light in August* makes Joe Christmas, a thirty-three-year-old scapegoat, its protagonist, while *The Sound and the Fury* vaguely follows the occurrences of Easter week. There are many more writers who find the basic fabric of Christianity stimulating material for fiction.

An important point to consider is that Greene reflects a widespread interest in religious themes within the limits of his technique and background. My problem in this study was not to define

Greene's religious beliefs, but rather to evaluate his success or failure in having used artistically and imaginatively the properties of Roman Catholicism. I therefore addressed myself to the task of searching out motifs and patterns—showing how Greene uses certain themes and modifies them, and to what purpose and with what effect. My discussion relies principally on internal evidence. By analyzing plots, characters, and situations, I have endeavored to define the basis of the appeal that both the "entertainments" and the novels have. I did not minimize such other considerations as symbolism and technique but attempted to show how these either dominated the religious theme or were controlled by it.

Since the religious theme becomes clearly apparent in the novels beginning with *Brighton Rock*, I have devoted much more space to Greene's publications since 1938, the date when this curious and fascinating book first appeared. Ultimately, I think, Greene's reputation will rest on the books written since 1938; and his contribution to English letters will be most clearly evidenced by them. I have gone through the early work, endeavoring to show how Greene's craftsmanship has been constantly improving, but how his thinking has remained fairly much the same. Part of the plan of this study is to show how Greene's Catholicism is not one stance, but a variety of stances—not always, perhaps, compatible with the strictest and narrowest interpretations of his faith. The works before 1938, it seems to me, are of interest not only as fictions but also as preliminary sketches and as tentative efforts for those more serious works that beguile and enchant Greene's readers. And, of course, I am enthusiastic about Greene—he has enlarged the scope of the English novel.

I have also endeavored to show in the opening chapter the economic and social factors that are common to many novels originating in the 1930's and the 1940's. I have done this for two reasons: first, to show how Greene is very much of his era; second, to show how in his own way he reacts to the forces of tradition of English literary history. So much emphasis has been put on his Roman Catholicism that many overlook the fact that there is a considerable body of English letters that concerns itself with faith and loss of faith. It might be objected that this chapter is overly long; and I agree. Yet I think that the effort is justified because Greene's place in the stream of English fiction can be more readily seen against a panoramic view. Although Greene is very much in the current Continental literary swing, constantly challenging comparison with those other writers who make use of religiously oriented subject matters, he is first and last an English novelist.

Many parallels have been drawn between Greene and Mauriac, and many of these provoke analysis. I have tried to show how these two writers are alike, concentrating specifically on what Greene has learned from Mauriac, how Greene has improved as a craftsman from understanding and appreciating the skills of his French contemporary.

There is much more that needs to be done: a comprehensive study of Greene's sources; an examination of the spirit of place in his works; and a thorough analysis of his symbolism and of his peoples' names. An interesting study could be made of the influence of Freud, of Kafka, of Proust; of Dickens and Conrad and James and Ford Madox Ford, for that matter. But I have left these problems for others.

I should like to thank The Viking Press and William Heinemann, Ltd., for permission to quote passages of Greene's texts from their editions. I should also like to thank Professor Maurice Beebe of *Modern Fiction Studies* for permission to use his Bibliography of Greene studies, printed in the Autumn 1957 issue of that periodical. And I should also like to thank him for having published in his magazine a preliminary study of *Brighton Rock*.

I should also like to thank Professor John Pick of *Renascence* for having published a preliminary study of Greene's entertainments and of *The Heart of the Matter* in that periodical; and also Mr. Robert Evans and Mr. William Jerome Crouch of the University of Kentucky Press for having published a preliminary study of the Green-Mauriac affiliation in their collection of Graham Greene criticism.

I should also like to thank Miss Sylvia Bowman and Miss Joan Sedgwick for their kindness and consideration in going over the manuscript; Professor Paul Wiley of the University of Wisconsin, without whose encouragement this study would never have been started; Professor Harold Watts of Purdue University, who read the manuscript and made many helpful suggestions; Professor Merrill May of Purdue University, who never said anything unkind about Greene; Miss Margaret Sullivan of the Purdue Libraries, who found several "irrevocably lost" books for me; and

Preface

Mrs. Joanna Comen and Mrs. V. E. Gibbens, who did the typing. I should also like to thank the Purdue Research Foundation for a summer grant that enabled me to do most of the writing that is now this study.

But most of all I should like to thank my friend Dr. Edward Nehls of Boston College for all that he has taught me about contemporary literature and, most especially, about Greene.

A. A. De Vitis

Purdue University
October, 1963

Contents

Chronology

1904   Graham Greene born October 2, in Berkhamsted, England, the fourth of six children.

1922-   Attended Balliol College, Oxford; edited *Oxford Outlook*.
1925

1925   Publication of *Babbling April*, poems.

1926   Employed by Nottingham *Journal*, without salary.

1926   Formally entered Catholic Church.

1926-   Subeditor for the London *Times*.
1930

1927   Marriage to Vivien Dayrell-Browning.

1929   Publication of *The Man Within*, his first novel.

1930   Publication of *The Name of Action*, later withdrawn.

1931   Publication of *Rumour at Nightfall*, later withdrawn.

1932   Publication of *Stamboul Train*, his first thriller; entitled *Orient Express* in the United States.

1934   Publication of *It's a Battlefield*, a novel.

1935   Publication of *The Basement Room*, a collection of stories.

1935   Publication of *England Made Me*, a novel; entitled *The Shipwrecked* in the United States.

1935-   Film critic for the *Spectator*.
1939

1936   Trip to Liberia, followed by *Journey Without Maps*, an account of his travels.

1936   Publication of *A Gun For Sale*, an entertainment; entitled *This Gun For Hire* in the United States.

1938   Publication of *Brighton Rock*, the first of the religiously oriented novels.

1938   Trip to Mexico; observations of Tabasco and Chiapas.

1939   Publication of *The Confidential Agent*, an entertainment.

1939   Publication of *The Lawless Roads*, an account of the Mexican voyage; entitled *Another Mexico* in the United States.

1940   Publication of *The Power and the Glory*, a novel; entitled *The Labyrinthine Ways* in the United States.

1940-
1941   Literary editor for the *Spectator*.

1941-
1946   Employed by Foreign Office; duty in Africa.

1943   Publication of *The Ministry of Fear*, an entertainment.

1947   Publication of *Nineteen Stories*.

1948   Publication of *The Heart of the Matter*, a novel.

1950   Publication of *The Third Man* and *The Fallen Idol*, both entertainments.

1951   Publication of *The Lost Childhood and Other Essays*.

1951   Publication of *The End of the Affair*, a novel.

1953   Publication of *The Living Room*, Greene's first drama.

1954   Publication of *Twenty-One Stories*.

1954-
1955   Trip to Indochina.

1955   Publication of *Loser Takes All*, an entertainment.

1955   Publication of *The Quiet American*, a novel.

1957   Publication of *The Potting Shed*, a drama.

1958   Publication of *Our Man in Havana*, an entertainment.

1959   Publication of *The Complaisant Lover*, a drama.

1959   Trip to Belgian Congo.

1961   Publication of *A Burnt-Out Case*, a novel.

1961   Publication of *In Search of a Character: Two African Journals*, accounts of two trips taken at different times.

1963   Publication of *A Sense of Reality*, stories.

Graham Greene

CHAPTER 1

The Literary Heritage

BEFORE the Industrial Revolution those living in the civilized world could easily assure themselves of the existence of God. They could prove it by the Bible, the document that offered written proof of a benevolent and omnipotent Deity operating in the world of men. But in the 1840's, 1850's, and 1860's these same believers saw a new scientific spirit open up illimitable vistas of geologic time and unmeasured eras of evolutionary change, all incompatible with the neatly ordered chronology of Bible narrative. The methods of historical criticism and the careful and scientific investigation of texts called into question the authenticity of the Bible as the word of God.

Man began to doubt that God had created the world in six days and rested on the seventh. Religion found itself in head-on collision with science. To accept the validity of a scientific approach to Truth was to deny the traditional wisdom of the Church. To make matters worse, this new scientific spirit was transforming the earth itself—the visible exponent of God—into a battleground where the banner "Survival of the fittest," was that to which all forms of human life gave heed. Wordsworth in the early 1800's had been able to describe his feelings about nature in reverential and ecstatic terms:

> —*Brook and road*
> *Were fellow travellers in this gloomy Pass,*
> *And with them did we journey several hours*
> *At a slow pace. The immeasurable height*
> *Of woods decaying, never to be decayed,*
> *The stationary blasts of waterfalls,*
> *And in the narrow rent, at every turn,*
> *Winds thwarting winds bewildered and forlorn,*
> *The torrents shooting from the clear blue sky,*

The rocks that muttered close upon our ears,
Black drizzling crags that spake by the wayside
As if a voice were in them, the sick sight
And giddy prospect of the raving stream,
The unfettered clouds and region of the heavens,
Tumult and peace, the darkness and the light—
Were all like workings of one mind, the features
Of the same face, blossoms upon one tree,
Characters of the great Apocalypse,
The types and symbols of Eternity,
Of first, and last, and midst, and without end.[1]

Tennyson—having read Charles Lyell's *Principles of Geology* (1830), having anticipated Darwin's *The Origin of Species* (1859), having followed the disputes of the Oxford Movement, and having been completely disillusioned with the scientific progress which he had seen as compensation for social ills in the first "Locksley Hall" (1842)—could find little in nature that bespoke goodness or peace. Nature in *In Memoriam* (1850) he saw as "red in tooth and claw"; and, in the second "Locksley Hall" (1886), he lamented the order of the world in which materialism seemed the criterion of progress: "Chaos, Cosmos! Cosmos, Chaos! who can tell how all will end! / Read the wide world's annals, you, and take their wisdom for your friend." [2] Tennyson's discouragement reflects that of all serious thinking Victorians. They understood that science had bereft them of God and had offered Chaos in return.

I

All, however, was not despair in the face of materialistic progress. Jeremy Bentham came to the problems of his time with an analytical and critical acumen that promised the "greatest good for the greatest number." [3] He denied the value of everything that he could not perceive with his senses, and he based his criticism of society on what could be tangibly improved. Bentham's view of man was not, however, a Romantic one.[4] Seeing all pleasure as a concomitant of pain, he believed that man's unimpaired search for pleasure was the end of life and that the amount of pleasure earned became the yardstick of progress. This calculus of hedonism, as it has come to be known, denied that morality had anything to do with God. It preached, instead, that morality was man made: It had been created by society, not inherited from God. Since this was so, Bentham thought, morality was a relative consideration and easily subject to modification; it could be changed to suit the demands of a materialistic, industrial world. Man, having dismissed the idea of God, could be as ruggedly individual as he liked so long as he secured the greatest amount of pleasure for himself. There seemed no other sanction for pleasure but the gratification of the individual lust.

"From the winter of 1821, when I first read Bentham," wrote John Stuart Mill in his *Autobiography,* "I had what might be called an object in life; to be a reformer of the world." And Mill went on to describe the feeling that overwhelmed him: that with Bentham a new era in thought had begun and that all previous moralists were superseded.[5]

Mill, however, came to see the fallacy of Bentham's argument, and insisted on defining the quality of pain and pleasure as well as the quantity. He accepted Bentham's three classifications of the world—the social order, the physical order, and the political order—but to them he added a fourth order of his own: the moral order or the sanction of conscience. He pictured conscience not as a God-given restriction on the activities of man but as the voice of society speaking through the individual: "It is only in a highly artificialized condition of human nature that the notion grew up, or, I believe, ever could have grown up, that goodness was natural . . . because only after a long course of artificial education did good sentiments become so habitual, and so predominant over bad, as to arise unprompted when occasions called for them." [6] And again he wrote, "Conformity to nature has no connection at all with right and wrong." [7]

Mill saw that the unhappiness of the individual might infringe on the happiness of others, and that it was the order of society that spoke through the conscience. He believed with Bentham that the best government was that which governed least, but he was forced to admit that the state had to exercise some curtailment of individual liberty to secure the common welfare. At the end of his life he came to advocate government ownership of industry. As a *laissez-faire* liberal, he found the greatest scope for individual expression in an untrammeled spirit of adventure and enterprise; as a thinking individual who could not accept the idea of God in his analysis of conscience, he found it necessary to accept the fact that something had to control the mass of humanity, for it would not control itself. And that control, he thought, could be the state itself.[8]

In 1859 was published one of the most important documents of the Victorian period, *The Origin of Species*. Charles Darwin insisted throughout his life that this document advanced an hypothesis as to the probable origin of the species, and he insisted that the theory was valid only insofar as his biological researches were concerned. Many, however, saw Darwinism as a sanction for a blind materialistic view of the universe. Herbert Spencer in *First Principles* (1862) pictured evolution as a necessity. He had read and appreciated Hegel, and he had combined the Hegelian dialectic with the principles of evolution. He concluded that through evolution the species must eventually become perfect.[9] From Darwin's biological theory Spencer developed a metaphysic which accounted for the whole universe. He saw matter going from indefinite, incoherent homogeneity to a definite, coherent heterogeneity. In other words, he saw matter becoming more complex as it evolved through time. Progress he saw as an impenetrable mystery, and he preached that nothing could thwart the evolutionary process. Like Bentham and Mill, he fought against trammeling the individual spirit, for he thought that moral restrictions would impede the evolutionary process. Spencer allowed, however, for the possibility of a god-like principle, the unknowable.

Thomas Henry Huxley, brilliant and trained in the empirical school, saw Darwin attacked by such people as "Soapy" Wilberforce, the Bishop of Oxford, who found the idea of evolution distasteful to his aesthetic as well as to his moral sense.[10] The Bishop of Oxford contended that Darwin did not understand the Bible and that he consciously sought to undermine religious conviction. In going to Darwin's defense, Huxley earned for himself the title of Darwin's "bulldog." (The bulldog delivered his famous lecture *The Physical Basis of Life* in Edinburgh in 1868.) He succeeded, to his own satisfaction, in discarding the religious trappings of Christian belief; but he retained its morality. He had an unbounded faith in science and felt certain that the truth could be seen by all, even by the layman to whom he presented his case. Huxley adopted the scientific method and, like Spencer, adapted it to society.[11] He agreed with Mill (and with Bentham) that conscience was a moral order. He pictured nature as Tennyson saw it, "red in tooth and claw," and civilization as man's protest against the forces of nature. However, he conceded that it might be possible for a God of Creation to exist, that it would be a fine thing if it were so; but he admitted that none of the facts pointed to such a conclusion. By allowing himself and his followers the luxury of an inquiring spirit, Huxley popularized agnosticism. No clearer link can be found between the pessimistic spirit of the nineteenth century and the doubting temper of the twentieth than between the work of Thomas Henry Huxley and the works of Julian and Aldous, his grandsons.

In France, Saint-Simon dreamed of a perfect civilization based on reason. He saw the scientific spirit replacing the religious. His chief protégé, Auguste Comte,[12] agreed with his teacher and defined three separate stages in the evolutionary process: the theological stage or the stage of myth; the metaphysical stage in which ethical values prevailed; and the positive stage in which laws could be advanced without the necessity of explaining causes, the stage in which truth had been arrived at by the scientific method. These three stages corresponded to the period of childhood innocence, the speculative period of youth, and the reasoning maturity of age. It was in the scientific stage—the positive stage—that Comte saw man as having outgrown the previous, primitive stages. In the positive period man looked at what he had learned through scientific investigation and relied on knowledge of things seen. Laws in the positive stage could be formulated without reference to causes. Through such reasoning Comte subjected reality—society—to the laws of the exact sciences; and he helped produce the science of society, which we know today as sociology.

The science of society, indeed, became his dominant concern, for he was primarily interested in the dynamic and static forces that were obvious in the phenomenal world. Like Mill, Spencer, and Huxley, he came upon the problem of morality and ethics. He wondered why man in a scientific, materialistic culture should be concerned with human welfare. The answer to his question had previously been religion and God. In his system of Positivism, however, society had long outgrown the theological stage, the first stage in the evolutionary process. Comte could not affirm the values of Christianity because such an affirmation would deny that the positive stage had been reached. So he invented the religion of humanity.

In human relations, Comte decided, the intellect is often subject to the emotions. Since society makes possible the continuation of the species and thereby guarantees immortality of a sort, society is in itself an object of worship. Society became for the Positivists a deity. To this new religion Comte added ritual akin to that of the Catholic Church; he adopted saints and ceremony; and he promised the perpetuation of the race. In Frederick Harrison,[13] he found a successor; and, through Harrison, the philosophy spread widely among the English intelligentsia. Such eminent Victorians as Harriet Martineau, George Henry Lewes, and George Eliot were affected.

Positivism found a particularly brilliant exponent in George Eliot, for she was revolting against conventional morality. In *Middlemarch* (.1872), Eliot portrayed the spirit of materialism rampant in the society of which she was a member. She watched Rosamond Vincy marry the idealistic young doctor, Lydgate, and ruin his career by insisting on the material advantages she thought her position as a doctor's wife merited. In her portrait of Farebrother, George Eliot pictured an English clergy grown inert; and she defined Victorian hypocrisy—the seeming acceptance of religious values—in her penetrating analysis of Bulstrode.

Earlier, in 1859, the same year that saw the publication of *The Origin of Species, Adam Bede* had appeared. The temper of *Adam Bede*[14] was quite different from that of *Middlemarch*. In *Adam Bede*, George Eliot had defined with particular brilliance the rise of Wesleyanism or Methodism in England. John Wesley and his followers distrusted the Anglican Church and placed an emphasis on personal response to the word of God, stressing that all men are of equal value to God. Through the preacher, Dinah, George Eliot described the industrial cities where people worked for something less than living wages. To these people Methodism offered the reward of another life. Through Hetty Sorrel, the infanticide, she described the infinite value of the meanest soul. George Eliot chronicled with admiration a religion that offered so much humanity as its token. In *Middlemarch*, however, the materialistic spirit was dominant. The promise of religion had failed. George Eliot neglected the more human aspects of life and expended her energies on a coldly intellectual analysis of provincial life adapting itself to the positive phase of Comtian evolution.[15]

The Oxford Movement (begun in 1833) proposed to investigate the bases of Anglican belief in God. John Henry Newman and Edward Pusey, John Keble and R. H. Froude, all Anglicans, investigated the findings of the "historical" criticism. Basically the Oxford Movement was an attempt to reaffirm the dogmas of Christian belief in the Anglican Church. It was the purpose of the investigators to evaluate the historical documents comprising the Bible and to arrive at conclusions concerning the validity of Anglican belief. The average Victorian had relied on a literal, or fundamental, reading of the Bible to sustain his religious convictions; but as a result of the critical investigations of Biblical texts in Tübingen, Germany, the authenticity of the word of God seemed called into question. This "higher criticism," following a method of scrupulous textual analysis, had discovered discrepancies in the Biblical narratives. It discovered many historical contexts for the books of the Bible and not a unique context as people had hitherto supposed. It also discovered several hands in the writing of a single book.

"As soon as I saw the hitch in the Anglican argument, during my course of reading in the summer of 1839," wrote Newman in his autobiography, "I began to look about, as I have said, for some ground which might supply a controversial basis for my need." [16] Sustaining an insistent will to believe, Newman concluded that his faith was founded on dogma—the traditional wisdom of the past. He came to believe that the Bible was not a complete unit in itself, and he accepted the fact that many independent hands had had a part in its formulation. In all matters of dispute he referred to the writings of the Church fathers, and in this manner he was able to maintain his belief in God. Newman discovered, too, that the Anglican Church was an offshoot of the Roman Catholic Church, for which he could trace an Apostolic succession. It became inevitable that he should renounce his Anglicanism and adopt Roman Catholicism.[17] At the same time, influenced by Newman's decision to adopt the Roman persuasion, Gerard Manley Hopkins wrestled with his soul and wrote some of the most beautiful poetry of the century. Not until Robert Bridges printed his work, however, did Hopkins make an impression—and that impression was made on the poets of the first third of the twentieth century.

The Oxford Movement—which Newman led capably until he disgraced himself with his Anglican confederates—represented in itself an attack on the Utilitarianism of Bentham and Mill; it advocated the spiritual values over the material and insisted on the reality of God. Unfortunately, the split between Newman and the others diverted attention from the real mission of the movement; and, paradoxically, it hastened the decline of faith in the Anglican Church.

Matthew Arnold saw society at an impasse; the world once founded on faith was no longer extant, and he saw himself "Wandering between two worlds, one dead, / The other powerless to be born." [18] In "Dover Beach" he specifically lamented the decline of traditional belief:

> *The Sea of Faith*
> *Was once, too, at the full, and round earth's shore*
> *Lay like the folds of a bright girdle furled.*
> *But now I only hear*
> *Its melancholy, long, withdrawing roar,*
> *Retreating, to the breath*
> *Of the night-wind, down the vast edges drear*
> *And naked shingles of the world.* (21-28)

In *Culture and Anarchy* (1869), he reflected the contemporary disturbances incident to the decline of religion and the rise of the materialistic spirit. In it he made his famous distinctions between the Populace, the Barbarians, and the Philistines, and labeled all that was gross and materialistic as the triumph of Philistinism. Since religion was no longer a suitable answer to social ills, he saw the conflict narrowed down to one between Anarchy and its only effective opponent, Culture. Culture he defined as a compound of Hebraism and Hellenism: moral zeal guiding the free play of intelligence. He understood that those who had insisted on a fundamentalist reading of the Bible had failed to distinguish between poetic metaphor and poetic directness; that the Bible, nevertheless, insisted on certain cultural values which he defined as "Sweetness and Light." In *Culture and Anarchy* he sought to replace a faith in God with a faith in the accumulated wisdom of the past. He saw the Philistine faith in machinery as an outgrown and misdirected aspect of Hebraism; it was Hebraism without the long-range perspective afforded by Hellenism, by Sweetness and Light.[19]

Culture and Anarchy is Arnold's answer to the Benthamite ideal that the individual is to move unrestrained in the world of affairs. Like Bentham and Mill, Arnold felt that the necessary restraints on the individual were not those of God and religion but of Society—of Culture. *Culture and Anarchy* remains a key document in the history of Victorian doubt and despair since it offered a positive cure for the ills of industrialism. The pursuit of perfection was Arnold's approximation to the perfection of God, for belief in God seemed untenable in the Victorian circles in which he moved.

In his condemnation of Philistinism, the materialistic standards of the rising bourgeoisie, Arnold hit directly at such believers in material progress as Thomas Babington Macaulay, who put an unbounded faith in the progress of industry. But Macaulay was not so blind as to refuse to accept the fact of national discontent.[20] The Corn Law agitations, Chartism, and the various reform leagues were to him symbolic of the general unrest. He believed, however, that there was progress precisely because there was discontent. He believed that if men were perfectly satisfied with their state there would be no wish for improvement. In his *History of England,* the first two volumes of which appeared in 1848, he described the affluence of the English nation since the time of Charles II. He tabulated increases in the national revenue, gloried in the developments of the English military system, and exulted in the discovery and exploitation of mineral resources. Macaulay's was more than anything else a childlike wonder over the industrial achievements of his age. He saw the will of God manifesting itself in the ever-increasing comforts it accorded the rising bourgeoisie. In his personal religious thinking he tended to agnosticism; but he would not admit any derogation of churchly duty, for to do so would be to deny the *status quo* of which he thoroughly approved.

Thomas Carlyle, the most vehement of the Victorian thinkers, saw the rising spirit of the materialistic-minded middle class, and he deplored it. He saw the same social ills that Bentham and Mill had tried to ameliorate. Carlyle set about to refute the hedonistic calculus and to reaffirm "the imperishable dignity of man." In *Sartor Resartus*, he facetiously described himself going through a period of blind scientific determinism; but one day, while walking down the Rue St. Antoine de l'Enfer in Paris, he learned not to be afraid of fear. He learned to affirm the basic dignity of man. From an everlasting no, he passed into the center of indifference and finally to an everlasting affirmation of the place of God in the real world.

In *Sartor Resartus*, Carlyle defined his theory of Clothes, indicating in his own humorous fashion his belief that all social institutions were merely symbols of ultimate realities. In *Past and Present* (1843), he acutely analyzed the ills of society, and he asked the riddle of the Sphinx: How could England be so wealthy and yet so poor? He saw a nation dying of inanition because man had forgotten the place of God in life and his responsibility to his brother. Carlyle saw materialistic progress as Midas wealth—a wealth that did no one any good; the workhouses were full of the poor, and there was starvation in the midst of plenty. Men "have forgotten the right Inner True," he said, "and taken up with the Outer Sham True. . . . Foolish men mistake transitory semblances for eternal fact." [21] Carlyle insisted on the supernatural aspect of life, on supernaturalism in the natural order; and this supernaturalism led him to a pronouncement on the duty of man in the real world. He made Duty, borrowing a phrase from Kant, a Categorical Imperative; and he insisted on the necessity of work.[22] Distrusting the *laissez-faire* state and instinctively distrusting the individual's competence in governing himself, he saw hope for the world in the selection of appropriate heroes. He deemed it necessary to develop an eye for talent, so that an Aristocracy of Talent could be developed to direct the spiritual as well as material aims of society. He preferred to think of the leader as a hero; and because of the faith he placed in the hero-leader, Carlyle seems in the light of recent history a proto-Fascist.

Carlyle could not agree with Macaulay that matter transcends mind and that man was put on earth to be happy. He believed instead that the measure of man's humanity accounted for his unhappiness and also for his greatness. But Carlyle's affirmation of the place of God in the world indicates an optimistic faith in religious values.

Robert Browning is often characterized by the little song from

Pippa Passes—"God's in his heaven— / All's right with the world." This is, however, Pippa's song. Browning did believe in God; he was aware of the theory of evolution; and he kept in his own way abreast of the scientific advances of his time. In "Caliban upon Setebos" he made reference to Darwin's hypothesis that man and ape descended from a common ancestor and pictured Caliban's distrust and fear of an anthropomorphic God. In "Rabbi Ben Ezra" he took up the standard of faith to refute the hedonism of Fitzgerald's *Rubáiyát*. In "La Saisaz," however, he defined most clearly his religious convictions, which are indeed optimistic, but not blindly so: "I must say—or choke in silence—'howsoever came my fate, / Sorrow did and joy did nowise,—life well weighed,— preponderate.'"[23] His mature appraisal of life was not that of a blind optimist; he sought redress for the sufferings of this world in one beyond it. In the "Epilogue" to *Asolando* he reaffirmed his faith in the struggle and his belief in the ultimate triumph of good over evil.

With the decline of orthodox religion, although such writers as Carlyle and Browning maintained a belief in it in their own peculiar ways, the English were left open to all sorts of strange beliefs and esoteric cults. Madame Helena Blavatsky found a suitable and wealthy clientele for her Theosophist teachings. William Butler Yeats fell under her sway, nor did he ever fall completely out from it. Daniel Dunglas Hume (or Home), an American spiritualist came into prominence and made such converts as Bulwer Lytton and Elizabeth Barrett Browning.[24] Perhaps because of her ill health, Mrs. Browning was easy prey to those teachings that not only promised but also seemed to verify a life after death. She attended spiritualist meetings religiously while in Florence, and when in England she made it her practice to be present at any séance which her husband would allow her to attend.[25] Completely distrustful of these mediums, Browning wrote "Mr. Sludge, the Medium" to demonstrate to her the absurdity of believing in charlatans. Charles Dickens, too, was highly scornful of the occult. Yet in *A Christmas Carol* (1843) and in *Oliver Twist* (1838) he made use of the supernatural as thematic material,[26] and there are elements of the occult apparent in his unfinished last novel, *The Mystery of Edwin Drood*. Hume was investigated in the laboratory by the eminent scientist, Sir William Crookes, who almost ruined his reputation by validating Hume's phenomena.[27] Partially because of occultists of the order of Hume and Madame Blavatsky, the Theosophical Society was formed; its purpose was to investigate, invalidate, and accredit, if necessary, the "miracles" produced by these gifted individuals and to study seriously their beliefs.

Charles Dickens in his later novels came to evaluate more keenly than ever before the social ills of his time.[28] In *Bleak House* (1853), he portrayed the slum area of Tom all Alones, and he campaigned for the regulation of chancery laws. The most interesting of these later novels from the perspective of the rise of materialism is *Hard Times* (1854). From Mrs. Elizabeth Gaskell, the author of *Mary Barton* (1848) and *North and South* (1855), Dickens got the idea of portraying a typical Victorian industrialist community.[29] In Gradgrind—with his constant emphasis on Facts, Facts, Facts—he satirized the spirit of Benthamite Utilitarianism. Through Bounderby, the rugged individualist, he portrayed *laissez-faire* in action and its effects on the simple working people like Stephen Blackpool. The regenerative figure of Sissy Jupe moves through the novel emphasizing the beauties of the natural order. The world of *Hard Times* is, however, a godless one.[30]

Thomas Hardy derived materials for his poems from his inability to reconcile himself to the loss of a benevolent God. For his pessimistic attitude, he found philosophic confirmation in the writings of Schopenhauer and von Hartmann.[31] Unable, however, to deny completely the existence of a superior intelligence, he formulated a poetic framework in which he saw a cosmological process contradicting an ethical process. Hardy conceived of this cosmological process as a blind, impotent force which had unconsciously allowed for the creation of man, and he believed that this created man had slowly evolved into a state of sentience out of all proportion to his worth in the evolutionary scale. All the natural processes, which Wordsworth and the Romantics had found so expressive of the Deity, Hardy conceived of as "subaltern" to this blind, impotent force which in *The Dynasts* (1903, 1906, 1908) he came to call the Immanent Will. The only hope that Hardy would allow himself in the world was that this Will might eventually evolve into sentience as man himself had done, that it would realize its responsibility in having put man on the earth and, possibly, remedy the human predicament:

> *There seemed a strangeness in the air,*
> *Vermillion light on the land's lean Face:*
> *I heard a voice from I know not where:—*
> *"The Great Adjustment is taking place."* [32]

He saw right disestablishing wrong in this great readjustment of values, but he saw little hope in his lifetime. Tess, in *Tess of the D'Urbervilles* (1891) had to admit to her little brother that they lived in a blighted universe. Tess falls prey to the Immanent Will, as does the hero of *Jude the Obscure* (1895), for there is no provision made in the cosmos for such as they who brave the powers of creation. Orthodox religion offered no solace for Tess and Jude since it could not offer an acceptable belief in God. Thomas Hardy, indeed, bridges the Victorian period and the first quarter of the twentieth century.

In the 1890's the aesthetes came into prominence, and then the decadents. They decided, in the light of the materialistic advances of society, that there was no sense in creating art for society's sake and that art should be "art for art's sake." Symonds and Wilde, Symons and Johnson, Rossetti for a time, Swinburne and Pater all burned appropriately with hard gemlike flames while they wrote delicately turned lays and virelays, ballades and rondeaus, about Nankin plates, about jaded passions, about writing poems, and about spleen. Davidson and Thompson wrote about heaven and hell and about cities of dreadful night. ("Hélas," mourned Oscar Wilde; he was so bored!)

William Butler Yeats for a time fell under the influence of the aesthetes. He saw the world as they did—devoid of tradition. He viewed with alarm a society becoming more and more materialistic, and in his early poetry he found value only in words:

> *The woods of Arcady are dead,*
> *And over is their antique joy;*
> *Of old the world on dreaming fed;*
> *Grey Truth is now her painted toy;*
> *Yet still she turns her restless head:*
> *But O, sick children of the world,*
> *Of all the many changing things*
> *Of dreary dancing passed us whirled,*
> *To the cracked tune that Chronos sings,*
> *Words alone are certain good.*[33]

In his search for a tradition Yeats looked everywhere and finally settled on the olden glories of Ireland, glories preserved by aristocratic families such as Lady Gregory's and symbolized in her home at Coole. In time he came to formulate a poetic system similar to those of Spengler and Hegel but basing his partially on the spirit communications received through his wife. He also came to advocate the permanence of art, and he sought to retire into the "artifice of eternity." Speaking about Shelley, Yeats wrote in *Discoveries* about his own concern for tradition and about his ideas concerning the permanence of art in a chaotic period of history:

All symbolical art should be out of a real belief, and that it cannot do so in this age proves that this age is a road and not a resting place for the imaginative arts . . .

Lyrical poems even when they but speak of emotions common to all need, if not a spiritual belief like the spiritual arts, a life that has leisure for itself, and a society that is quickly stirred by the emotions of others. All circumstance that makes emotion at once dignified and visible, increases the poet's power, and I think that is why I have always longed for some stringed instrument and a listening audience not drawn out of the hurried streets but from a life where it would be natural to murmur over again the singer's thought.[34]

The winding stair became for him the symbolic means of reaching perfection; it led to the battlements of the Tower. But the Tower was half dead at the top, for only death, it seems, could bring him to that fullness whose quest he made his poetic search.

The legacy of the nineteenth century to the early twentieth century was a world of disillusionment—a world bereft of hope in God, a dull land, a wasteland. The God of religion seemed to have retired from it. While Karl Marx sat quietly in the British Museum writing that religion was the opiate of the people, religion was in a real sense fighting a battle of survival. World War I deepened the sense of sterility and emphasized the feeling that God had fled from the world. Vera Brittain in her *Testament of Youth* describes the despondency she felt as she wrote to her fiancé, Roland, and received his letters in return. As the Battle of Loos wore on, Roland wrote:

"Let him who thinks war is a glorious golden thing, who loves to roll forth stirring words of exhortation, invoking Honour and Praise and Valour and Love of Country with as thoughtless and fervid a faith as inspired the priests of Baal to call on their slumbering deity, let him but look at a little pile of sodden gray rags that cover half a skull and a shin bone and what might have been its ribs, or at this skeleton lying on its side, resting half crouching as it fell, perfect but that it is headless, and with the tattered clothing still draped round it; and let him realize how grand and glorious a thing it is to have distilled all Youth and Joy and Life into a foetid heap of hideous putrescence! . . ." [35]

And she answered:

"When I think of these things . . . I feel that that awful Abstraction, the Unknown God, must be some dread and wrathful deity before whom I can only kneel and plead for mercy, perhaps in the words of a quaint hymn of George Herbert's that we used to sing at Oxford:

> Throw away thy wrath!
> Throw away thy rod!
> O my God
> Take the gentle path!" [36]

Hilaire Belloc and G. K. Chesterton maintained their belief in Roman Catholicism and in so doing revolted against the materialistic spirit of the times. Their influence was, however, for the moment. In such a study as André Maurois' *The Edwardian Era,* they are dismissed with a few summary sentences. Another critic, Shaw Desmond, characterizes them as writers who wrote "without convincing"; a reader would "have to be of their religious persuasion" to accept them wholeheartedly.[37]

May Sinclair defended idealism in the period. In 1917 she wrote *A Defence of Idealism: Some Questions and Conclusions.* She discussed the philosophies of Samuel Butler, Henri Bergson, Bertrand Russell, F. H. Bradley, and William James. In the Introduction she wrote: "I think it may be said that certain vulnerable forms of Idealism are things of the past; and that the new atomistic Realism is a thing of the future; at any rate of the immediate future. . . . I think that someday (which may be as distant as you please) the New Realism will grow old and die, and the New Idealism will be born again." [38]

The most important defender of the idealistic spirit, however, was George Bernard Shaw. Finding the materialism of the times an increasing problem, he dramatized it in one dilemma play after another. He used "Wilde's epigrammatic style to express serious ideas." [39] In 1921 Shaw wrote *Back to Methuselah* and portrayed a world in which idealism and contemplation became the ends of life. He rebelled against the neo-Darwinians and based his theory of evolution on Lamarck and Bergson. This evolution was "Creative," an answer to the philosophy of the Mechanists and the neo-Darwinians.[40]

But the prevailing temper of the first quarter of the century as far as the thinking individual was concerned seemed pessimistic. T. S. Eliot caught the feeling and defined the twentieth century in the most influential poem of the century, *The Waste Land* (1922). C. Day Lewis in *A Hope for Poetry* (1945), says of Eliot: "It is very much to Eliot's credit as a poet that he detected the death will in western civilization before it rose to the surface in the disillusionment of the later war years." [41] In *The Waste Land* Eliot, in terms of multiple myth, defined the contemporary world as a sterile land in which even death was meaningless. He saw the life-giving water gone from the earth and nothing but desert and lust and godlessness apparent. In "The Hollow Men" (1925) he wrote:

> *This is the dead land*
> *This is cactus land*
> *Here the stone images*
> *Are raised, here they receive*
> *The supplication of a dead man's hand*
> *Under the twinkle of a fading star.*[42]

In his poetry, however, Eliot, by defining the death wish, implied its opposite—the will to be reborn; and he established a pattern of conversion.[43] In "Ash Wednesday" (1930), he spoke of the purple of penance and prayed to God for courage to persist in the search for faith; he asked for the patience to learn discipline, to sit still. In *The Waste Land,* Eliot defined the sterility, the lust, and the pessimism of the twentieth century; in "Ash Wednesday," he moved into the penance advocated by orthodox religion—in his case, the Anglo-Catholic Church. He who had defined the waste land and made it the dominant motif in the literature of the 1920's and 1930's asserted in subsequent poems the values of orthodox belief and of the traditional wisdom of the Church.

In other words, Eliot rediscovered more than a century later many of the truths that the Romantics and the early Victorians had taken for granted, truths that the scientific materialism prevalent in the nineteenth century had pushed into the background. Wordsworth had felt instinctively and emotionally the beauty of God in nature; Shelley and Keats had felt in the depths of their souls that truth was beauty and beauty truth. The twentieth century, inheritor of the black determinism of the nineteenth, had to rise Phoenix-like to truth from the ashes of the pessimism of the previous era.[44] Tennyson had mirrored in his whole poetic output first the enthusiasm and then the disillusionment of his age. Thomas Hardy had formulated a poetic framework out of his inability to compensate for the loss of the God of orthodox religion. T. S. Eliot detected and defined the death wish in Western civilization; and he was the first important poet to emerge from the waste land through the gateway of Faith, the same Faith that had gone out with the tide of science in Arnold's "Dover Beach."

In the *Four Quartets* (1943), Eliot reached a fuller meaning, a stronger harmony, the peace that had been absent in the world for over a century. The garden and the laughter of the children became dominant over the desert and the laments of the people who existed in it. In "Burnt Norton," Eliot expressed a belief in humanity, in salvation out of life, out of time:

> *Love is itself unmoving,*
> *Only the cause and end of movement,*
> *Timeless, and undesiring*
> *Except in the aspect of time*
> *Caught in the form of limitation*
> *Between un-being and being.*
> *Sudden in a shaft of sunlight*
> *Even while the dust moves*
> *There rises the hidden laughter*
> *Of children in the foliage*
> *Quick now, here now, always—*
> *Ridiculous the waste sad time*
> *Stretching before and after.*[45]

II

Charles Ryder says in Evelyn Waugh's *Brideshead Revisited* (1945):

I had no religion. I was taken to church weekly as a child, and at school attended chapel daily, but, as though in compensation, from the time I went to my public school I was excused church in the holidays. The view implicit in my education was that the basic narrative of Christianity had long been exposed as a myth, and that opinion was now divided as to whether its ethical teaching was of present value, a division in which the main weight went against it; religion was a hobby which some people professed and others did not; at the best it was slightly ornamental, at the worst it was the province of "complexes" and "inhibitions"—catch words of the decade—and of the intolerance, hypocrisy, and sheer stupidity attributed to it for centuries. No one had ever suggested to me that these quaint observances expressed a coherent philosophic system and intransigeant historical claims; nor, had they done so, would I have been much interested.[46]

A few, like H. G. Wells, maintained faith in the machine. But, on the whole, the nineteenth century left to the twentieth a growing uneasiness in the face of the materialistic advances of science and the rising influence of the middle class. Moral and political ideas succumbed to the influence of Lenin and Marx, and the human personality found itself subjected to the analyses of Jung and Freud. T. S. Eliot detected the death wish in Western civilization, defined it, and set forth the most comprehensive set of symbols for characterizing the period of the early twentieth century. Few serious thinkers were able to maintain orthodox belief in the face of confusion or chaos. There was no place to turn, and it became fashionable to be psychoanalyzed in order to understand how the personality reflected the order of the day. In the late 1920's and early 1930's, there came a depression following upon the inflation and the mad good times of the post-World War I period. Economic catastrophe was a reality. The hopes of Shaw and the Fabians dimmed in the tide of Spanish Fascism, and, later, German totalitarianism. The predicament in which man found himself seemed beyond solution.

In the first quarter of the twentieth century, the concern was with form, style, and technique. Virginia Woolf in her criticism rebelled against the naturalism of the nineteenth century, and in *The Common Reader* (1925), she demonstrated clearly her anti-intellectual approach to literature. She preferred to analyze the text in the fashion of the late Romantics, dismissing the Victorian standards of scholarship and history. She watched Mrs. Dalloway through a day of her life, and in that one day she told her reader all he needed to know concerning her heroine. And Mrs. Dalloway's existence did not include God. She could feel sorry for Septimus Warren Smith, but the causes of his dilemma were primarily psychical, social, and economic; indeed, God had no place in the pattern of Mrs. Dalloway's thoughts. Lily Briscoe in *To the Lighthouse* (1927) concerned herself with the representation of Mrs. Ramsey as a splotch of paint on her canvas. Mrs. Ramsay sought to hold the moment of harmony at the dinner party, and for one moment it did occur to her to think of God. Graham Greene has said that the characters of Virginia Woolf "wandered like cardboard symbols through a world that was paper-thin." [47] Bernard Blackstone says of her religion: "Virginia Woolf's aversion from Christianity springs first . . . from her hatred of hypocrisy. It springs also from her sensitiveness to unpleasantness and pain. These things are, artistically, outside her scope. She knows they are there; and . . . she is even too acutely conscious of them. They contradict her vision of beauty and significance." [48]

E. M. Forster in *A Passage to India* (1924) and especially in *Howards End* (1910) described the Philistinism that Matthew Arnold had defined in *Culture and Anarchy*. The Schlegels he represented as Sweetness and Light, and Mr. Wilcox became material progress. In "Howards End," Mrs. Wilcox's home, Forster symbolized the forces of tradition. The unseen presence of Mrs. Wilcox hovering over the house speaks of God, but very obliquely. It is the tradition of "Howards End" that is important.[49]

Arnold Bennett and John Galsworthy plodded on in their realistic fashion, but their realism seemed to imply no God in the world. John Galsworthy's *The Forsyte Saga* (1922) moved the Forsytes out of the Victorian era, through the Edwardian lull, and into the twentieth century in which not even Soames's property was valuable any longer. Arnold Bennett's *The Old Wives' Tale* (1908) traced the development of two sisters in mundane, realistic description that often sprang into a vitality all of its own. But neither Sophia nor Constance paid any more than lip service to God.

A few like D. H. Lawrence reacted violently against the severe and unfeeling strictures of nineteenth-century religion. In his rebellion were contained the seeds of a religious search, for Lawrence sought to revitalize religion by returning to the springs of feeling. He looked in *The Plumed Serpent* (1926) for king-gods, and in *The Man Who Died* (1928), he took the Christ myth and infused his own ideas of sex into it. Christ, he decided, had not been a whole man because he had not found his polarity in woman. So Lawrence raised Him from the tomb and sent Him out searching for a complement. Lawrence found represented in the art and life of the Etruscans the epitome of civilization; and it was their appreciation of life, of vitality, of meaningful existence that he attempted to incorporate in his own final work.[50] He traveled the world looking for a race that still was expressive of dark and vital blood; and in Mexico he thought he found untrammeled feelings and vital meaning springing from a belief in the ancient gods of the Mexicans. Lawrence's search was a real one. Having inherited the disillusionment of the nineteenth century, he felt it necessary to find a substitute religion. That which he formulated, unfortunately, most people found distasteful, choosing to misunderstand his exaltation of sex.

James Joyce in Ireland rejected Irish Catholicism, and by doing so he turned himself, perhaps paradoxically, into the most Catholic of writers. In *A Portrait of the Artist as a Young Man* (1916), he traced his own spiritual awareness in the character of Stephen Dedalus; and, like Stephen, Joyce concluded that to remain faithful to his artistic vision he would have to leave Ireland. *Ulysses* (1922), his magnificent *tour de force,* worked in terms of classical myth; it traced Stephen's rebellion against his God and his country still further. Into *Ulysses* Joyce put all the paraphernalia of psychoanalysis, of Jung and Freud, and fused it with a stream-of-consciousness technique; and, once and for all, he indicated the limitations of that device in the soliloquies of Mollie and Leopold Bloom.

In the 1930's a group of poets picked up the threads of idealism and began to take stock; they looked about them and saw to what monstrous size the social organism had grown. W. H. Auden,

Stephen Spender, and C. Day Lewis began to advocate English Socialism. They preached decentralization of industry so that the social unit might be made smaller and man might again communicate with man. They sought to revitalize poetic metaphor by drawing images from the machine itself, and they tried to re-educate the masses to understand the dangers of capitalism. They claimed literary descent from Gerard Manley Hopkins, T. S. Eliot, Wilfred Owen, and D. H. Lawrence. From the ruins of nineteenth-century pessimism that had led those of the early twentieth century to wish for death, they sought for new meaning, a new order. They looked for a way out of the waste land. Eliot in his poetry had defined the era; they took up the battle from there. Meanwhile Eliot clarified his beliefs in his literary criticism.

In *After Strange Gods* (1934), Eliot showed himself aware of the confusion apparent in the writings of the nineteenth century. He praised George Eliot for her insights into human motivations, but he deplored her individualistic morals. He insisted that the writer, to be faithful to society, had to remain within an orthodox conception of history and tradition. He pointed out that when morals cease to be a matter of tradition and orthodoxy *personality* becomes alarmingly important.[51]

Eliot found Thomas Hardy's extreme emotionalism a symptom of decadence, for Hardy's personality was "uncurbed by any institutional attachment or by submissions to any objective beliefs. . . ."[52] And he deplored Lawrence's eccentricity in setting up for himself a system of gods opposed to the Church. To Lawrence, Eliot said, any spiritual force was good; and evil resided only in the absence of spirituality.[53]

Eliot, in other words, asserted the validity of the orthodox teachings of the Church. He found in the wisdom of the Church the answer to the ills of the waste land and a measure upon which to base one's spiritual awareness. Furthermore, Eliot thought it necessary that the artist point out the difference between good and evil, insisting that awakening men to the spiritual life was a very great responsibility: "It is only when they [men] are so awakened that they are capable of real Good, but . . . at the same time they become first capable of Evil."[54] The artist had become aware that art could not exist for itself alone.

The orthodox teachings of the Church found very real opponents in the political theories prevalent in the 1930's. William York

Tindall in *Forces in Modern British Literature: 1885-1946*, describes the influences that marked English literature after World War I: "Disenchantment and its effects, the cynical, the disgusting, and the grotesque, though products of the first World War, existed before it as products of science and bourgeois self-contemplation. With these effects came others, the comic, the ironic, and the fantastic, the last of which appears an attempt of the disenchanted to rediscover enchantment. Attitudes of disenchantment, found at their happiest in the work of Huxley and young Waugh, occur so abundantly that, like politics and religion, they discover the times." [55]

The 1930's continued to lament a world in which physics had displaced metaphysics and limited reality to matter. The return to the Church, paralleling the trend to Communism and Socialism, indicated a desire to reunite matter with spirit. It indicated the fact that religion was catching up with science: "The reunion of matter and spirit symbolized union of self and world and, beyond this, of the unconscious with the conscious. Religions offered ends and means." [56] The real opponents to the Church in the 1930's were the Fascist and Communist ideologies.

André Gide, in his *Journals* from 1928-1939, best typifies the attitudes that opposed the march back to the Church. In Arcachon on the tenth of August, 1930, he wrote in his journal: "The great grievance one can have against the Christian religion is that it sacrifices the strong to the weak. But that strength should strive to find its function in bringing help to weakness, how can one fail to approve this? [57]

The conflict was between a cult of power and a religion of love. To approve the teachings of the Church and to accept the teachings of Marx and Lenin seemed impossible, for love and violence were totally incompatible. Communism advocated strength and the strong man, whereas capitalism allowed for meekness and humility. Gide wrote in his journal for the ninth of January, 1933, in double-edged irony:

But I see only too well, alas, how and why capitalism and Catholicism are bound up together and the great advantage that capitalism can find in a religion that teaches a man whom society strikes on the right cheek to hold out the left, which benumbs the oppressed and soothes him with hopes of an afterlife, transfers rewards to a mystical place, and lets the oppressor enjoy a triumph which it persuades the oppressed to be but illusion. How could the man who knows that Christ said: "happy those that weep" fail to take advantage of Catholicism, and how could "those that weep" not accept submission if they know that "the last shall be first"? Theirs is the kingdom of God; the possessors leave it to them if it is well understood that those that weep will leave to the possessors the kingdom of this earth. Everything therefore is for the best and no one has anything to complain about. Christ remains on the side of the poor, to be sure; the rich leave him on their hands. The poor almost thank them for this. They know that they have "the better part." And probably Christ did not want this. In his time the social question could not be raised. Replying to a specious question, he said: "Render unto Caesar. . . ." So much has been rendered unto Caesar that there is nothing left for *him*. But the poor know that everything they give up here below will be "returned to them an hundred fold." One cannot imagine a better investment!

And the rich still find a way of conciliating Christ (or of reconciling themselves with him) by making a point of being "charitable." For, after all, they have kindness—which will allow them, they hope, while keeping all their advantages "here below," not to allow themselves to be dispossessed of all hope of still being, after death, on the right side.[58]

But Gide was forced to admit that there was value in tradition and that systems which endeavored to build by destroying had their limitations. It was absurd, Gide stated, to condemn the past in the name of the future and not to realize a filtration, a succession. He insisted that only by thrusting out a foothold into the past could the present spring into the future.[59] This statement, in all its force, coming from the advocate of the gratuitous act—the act committed for no real reason except to gratify the individual lust —indicates how far Gide had gone since his earliest works. The reliance on tradition, although Gide would never agree with the teachings of any church, indicates that the *enfant terrible* in his maturity came to realize the necessity of restricting individual conduct.

The Church, then, offered again a basis for real meaning in the world to those who would accept its teachings. Not only that, but religion suddenly became popular. The interest in psychoanalysis and Freud found a close rival in religion.[60] It became fashionable to become converted to either Anglicanism or Roman Catholicism. One was required to show an intense interest in the forms of worship to be in the literary swing. What is important, however, is that those writers who wrote about religion took their work seriously. They wrote for society, and they had a message to deliver. The message indicated how man could put his garden to rights and reclaim the desert waste it had become since Science had moved God out of the Church. Graham Greene and Aldous Huxley and Rex Warner and Evelyn Waugh and Christopher Isherwood and W. H. Auden and many more fell into the pattern of conversion.

The writers of the 1930's, following a pattern implied by T. S. Eliot in his own work and using the imagery and motifs of *The Waste Land,* looked about them and decided that something had to be done about society. They realized that their function as writers was an important one, and they realized that their responsibility was a serious one. Graham Greene wrote to Elizabeth Bowen and V. S. Pritchett:

> First I would say there are certain human duties I owe in common with the greengrocer or the clerk—that of supporting my family if I have a family, of not robbing the poor, the widow or the orphan, of dying if the authorities demand it (it is the only way to remain independent; the conscientious objector is forced to become a teacher in order to justify himself). These are our primitive duties as human beings. . . . I would say that if we do less than these, we are so much the less human beings and therefore so much the less likely to be artists. But are there any special duties I owe to my fellow victims bound for the Loire? I would like to imagine there are none, but I fear there are at least two duties the novelist owes—to tell the truth as he sees it and to accept no special privileges from the state.[61]

By "truth" Greene meant that the novelist had to describe accurately, and that the authenticity of his observations depended on the validity of the emotion he was describing. As far as his own writing is concerned, Greene took Cardinal Newman for his guide. As a Catholic he maintained, with Newman, that he had to write about good as well as evil and that it was the responsibility of the artist to awaken sympathetic comprehension not only for the evil but for the "smug, complacent, successful characters." [62]

Greene realized that it was the duty of the novelist to be a thorn in the side of orthodoxy, and perhaps a questioner of the complacent who accepted religious dogma blindly, in order to reawaken the reader to a comprehension of the essential mystery of life: "Sooner or later the strenuous note of social responsibility, of Marxism, of the greatest material good of the greatest number must die in the ear, and then perhaps certain memories will come back, of long purposeless discussions in the moonlight about life and art. . . ." [63] For Greene the writer "just as much as the Christian Church, is the defender of the individual." [64] Greene's own answer to Fascism and Communism is his Roman Catholicism. And it is his Roman Catholicism that informs his novels. Rex Warner, a writer of great stature and unappreciated skill, concurs with Greene's analysis of the function of the artist in society:

This is what may be called the political task of literature—to hold the mirror up to nature, to show men how they live and what is meant by their own words and manners, to investigate everything under the sun, to retain the tradition of the past, and to explore the future, to instruct, to criticize, to delight, to create and to reveal. In these activities, as in all others, the writer may be greatly helped or greatly hindered by the society in which he lives. The more he can co-operate with this society, the happier, as a rule, he will be. Yet, though his work is conditioned by his social group, it is not determined by it. And there is a sense in which it is true to say that his work must be, whether he is conscious of it or not, always disruptive of any State organization. For his loyalties as a writer are to something wider and deeper than any State can be. [65]

Graham Greene believes that the way out of the waste land is belief in God. He insists on the doctrines of his Church as a possible answer to the power and violence that characterize the political ideologies of our times. His personal convictions are matters of individual belief; yet what he says has universal meaning. He proposes a Bible of love and forgiveness, and he opposes it to the cult of the power addict. Ultimately he is a proponent of humanism, of dignity, and of right. His work has meaning because it transcends the limitations of his religious themes. Indeed, he is in his own way very much in the tradition of English letters.

CHAPTER 2

The Catholic as Novelist

IN *The Emperor's Clothes,* an attack on the dogmatic assertions
of writers who use religion as background and rationale for
their works, Kathleen Knott says about the novelist who writes
from a Roman Catholic point of view: "It seems to be much
easier for Catholic writers who are born Catholic, for instance
Mauriac, to stick to psychological truth than it is for converts.
This may be because it is much easier to ignore Catholic theory
when it is acquired below the age of reason. Anglo-Saxon writers
probably have a special disadvantage in this respect." [1]

Miss Knott aims her barb directly at Graham Greene and
Evelyn Waugh, both converts to Roman Catholicism, the former
in 1926 and the latter in 1930; and she goes on to observe that she
finds the situation described in Greene's *The Power and the Glory*
credible because the actions of the characters result from the
interplay between a sentimental-religious education and the concrete circumstances of socialistic, government intolerance. But for
The Heart of the Matter and *The End of the Affair* she has no
sympathy, finding the situations described in these books facti-
tious: "To be artistically satisfying the situation must be objec-
tively described. The author must not imply that, for esoteric
reasons, he knows more about the answers to the problem than
the characters do. You can write a human book about a Catholic
if you do not at the same time write a book about Catholic theories of human nature." [2] Indeed, Miss Knott puts her finger on
the point that has given rise to much of the controversy excited
by the religious provocations portrayed by both Greene and
Mauriac in their works.

Since the publication of *Brighton Rock* in 1938 the framework
of Greene's novels, with the exception of *The Quiet American*
(1955), has been Roman Catholicism. Writing for an audience

primarily Protestant in orientation, Greene has faced obstacles as a novelist that Mauriac, who acquired his religious training "below the age of reason," has not. Yet both these novelists have been faced with an identical problem regarding their artistic and religious integrity. Ultimately, both concern themselves with the capacity of the human heart for sacrifice and greatness within a world governed by a God who seems unreasonable, hostile, and oftentimes indifferent; and both concern themselves with the all-pervasive nature of grace, the incontestable mystery of good and evil, and the inability of man to distinguish between the two.

The fact, however, that these writers—one born a Roman Catholic, the other a convert to Roman Catholicism—deal with the predicaments of human beings within a framework of morality that is labeled Roman Catholicism does not necessarily mean that they are novelists who allow their appreciation of the orthodoxy of their beliefs to govern the artistic conception of their works. It would be just as foolish to label Homer a Greek theologian because Odysseus and Agamemnon are Greeks and concerned with the caprices of the deities. Furthermore, both Greene and Mauriac are conscious of the difficulties of their positions as artists and have written perceptively and persuasively on the nature of their responsibilities to both their craft and their faith. Both have been accused by their critics of "conniving" with the devil in portraying their themes.

Speaking within the defined limits of Thomistic philosophy, Jacques Maritain discusses in *Art and Scholasticism* the problem of evil in the world and the novelist's responsibility to his audience. The novelist's purpose, he says, is not to mirror life as the painter does, but to create the experience of it. The novel, of course, derives its rules of conduct from the real world; but, as a work of art, its validity depends on the quality of the life-experience it creates. It becomes the responsibility of the novelist to understand with what object he portrays the aspects of evil which form the materials of the true art work: "The essential question is *from what altitude* he depicts and whether his art and mind are pure enough and strong enough to depict it without connivance. The more deeply the modern novelist probes human misery, the more does it require super-human virtues in the novelist." [3]

According to Maritain the only writer who can be a complete

artist is a Christian, for only he has some idea of the potentialities of man and of the factors limiting his greatness. The Christian writer who approaches his craft honestly portrays the universal truths which are valid within a Christian configuration of morality and ethics. If the artist finds himself in too much sympathy with misery and suffering, his pity may lead him to censure the forces of divinity which make themselves apparent in the phenomenal world. Such art becomes destructive, even self-destructive, for it defeats any moral end. It is for this reason that Maritain finds the influence of Gide pernicious, for much of Gide's work exalts a gratuitous act without consideration of its moral and ethical ramifications. But neither Greene nor Mauriac, many of their Catholic readers insist, maintains a suitable "altitude."

Graham Greene has been accused by his critics and fans alike of "conniving" with the devil; he has been called a Manichaean, a Jansenist, a Quietist, an Existentialist, and other names as well. Many commentators have made an attempt to abstract his personal convictions from the world of his invention, insisting, understandably enough, on a prerogative of philosophical and religious speculation. But many of his commentators, critics, and fans have failed to understand the important fact that in his novels, and often in his entertainments, Greene describes a human condition, and that the experience of life developed within that human condition is not representative of a religious bias. Greene himself says in a letter to Elizabeth Bowen and V. S. Pritchett:

If I may be personal, I belong to a group, the Catholic Church, which would present me with grave problems as a writer were I not saved by my disloyalty. If my conscience were as acute as M. Mauriac's showed itself to be in his essay *God and Mammon*, I could not write a line. There are leaders of the Church who regard literature as a means to an end, edification. I am not arguing that literature is amoral, but that it presents a different moral, and the personal morality of an individual is seldom identical with the morality of the group to which he belongs. You remember the black and white squares of Bishop Blougram's chess board. As a novelist, I must be allowed to write from the point of view of the black square as well as of the white: doubt and even denial must be given their chance of self-expression, or how is one freer than the Leningrad group? [4]

In the novels since *Brighton Rock*, with the possible exception of *The Quiet American*, Greene creates an experience of life—

to use Maritain's phrase—in which the religion of the chief actors is Roman Catholicism. Like the people of Henry James, a writer whom Greene much admires, they make a place for themselves within the experience, exciting the pity and curiosity of the reader as they move within the boundaries of a problem that often seems to admit no earthly solution. If Greene were to force his people to react to the conditions in which they find themselves as good and true Catholics would, if the solution for their unhappiness were brought about in terms of the author's religious convictions, then indeed the results would be bad art— if art at all. But a novelist who retains his faith as a man can be allowed a point from which to explore evil. If a novelist glorifies good and refuses to recognize the beauty of evil, the beauty that Lucifer carried with him when he fell, and if the novelist attests only the validity of a religious dogma, he is, as Greene says, "a philosopher or religious teacher of the second rank." [5]

The fact is that Greene is primarily a novelist; he is neither a theologian nor a philosopher. In his book *In Search of a Character*, Greene says: "I would claim not to be a writer of Catholic novels, but a writer who in four or five books took characters with Catholic ideas for his material. Nonetheless for years—particularly after *The Heart of the Matter*—I found myself hunted by people who wanted help with spiritual problems that I was incapable of giving. Not a few of these were priests themselves." [6] Greene also states in his essay on Henry James that "The novelist depends preponderantly on his personal experience, the philosopher on correlating the experience of others, and the novelist's philosophy will always be a little lop-sided." [7]

Ultimately Greene concerns himself with the problems of good and evil not so much as they exist within the Catholic Church but as they exist in the great world. His novels deal primarily with the fall of man; and at least two of them, *The Power and the Glory* and *The Heart of the Matter*, afford the possibility of heroic action. Although Catholicism pervades the plots of his novels, Greene is not concerned in justifying the activities of his religion. Greene chooses to deal with the seedy, the unlikable, the unhappy —those in whom he feels the strange power of God. When he does choose to work with sainthood, his work suffers, as does perhaps *The End of the Affair*. Perhaps Mauriac explains the failure when he writes in *God and Mammon*:

Why should not we portray saints just as Benson, Foggazaro, Boumann and Bernanos did—or tried to do? On the other hand it could be maintained that on his point of sanctity the novelist loses his rights, for if he tries to write a novel about sanctity he is no longer dealing purely with men, but with the action of God on men—and this may be an extremely unwise thing to try to do. On this point it seems that the novelist will always be beaten by reality, by the saints who really have lived.[8]

When Greene is concerned with sin and the possibility of re-demption, he is at his best, choosing deliberately to create his experience of life in uncharted theological waters. But at the end of the life-experience he reestablishes his direction and relocates his port. To do this Greene uses a spokesman of the Church of which he is a member: the priest who comforts Rose at the end of *Brighton Rock*, Father Rank, who comforts Louise Scobie at the end of *The Heart of the Matter*, Father Browne in *The Living Room*. These characters are not merely plot contrivances, *dei ex machina*, as they at first appear; rather, they reestablish the ethical norms of behavior and a proper religious perspective after the passions of men have spent themselves. As in Elizabethan and Jacobean drama, order must be reestablished before the spectator can be released. In *Hamlet* the audience leaves the theater with the knowledge of Fortinbras' reestablishment of order in Denmark. The trick is one that Greene learned from his study of the drama, and he puts it to capital use in his melodramatic pieces.

Born in 1904, Graham Greene attended Berkhamsted School in Hertfordshire, about twenty-five miles northwest of London, where his father was a teacher. The elder Greene had left Oxford intending to become a lawyer but instead had become a school-master. The boy Graham, one of six children, hated the town and the school. To escape from the all-pervasive eyes of the school authorities, he took to solitary walks forbidden by the rules; once he ran away from the school and hid on the common where he was found by his sister. Of these early years, during which he tried several times to commit suicide, he has written poignantly in "The Lost Childhood" and "The Revolver in the Corner Cup-board." At seventeen he went to Oxford, ultimately taking a "second" in modern history. For six weeks, as a prank, he was a dues-paying member of the Communist Party. At the age of twenty he published his first book, *Babbling April*, a collection of

poems, now a collector's item, that owed much to his reading
of Edna St. Vincent Millay. After his graduation from Balliol, he
worked for a time as subeditor for the London *Times*. In 1927 he
married Vivien Dayrell-Browning, a Roman Catholic; the period
of his conversion is described in *The Lawless Roads*. The marriage
produced two children.

In 1929 Heinemann accepted the manuscript of his first novel,
The Man Within, which was well received by the critics in England but was a failure in the United States. This novel was followed by *The Name of Action* (1930) and by *Rumour at Nightfall*
(1931), two works that Greene has withdrawn from his bibliography and has encouraged his readers to forget. In 1932 *Stamboul
Train* was published, and Greene became a popular success. From
1935 to 1939 Greene was film critic for the *Spectator,* and this post
may account for the use of cinematographic techniques character-
istic of much of his early work. Greene has traveled extensively,
in Africa, in Mexico, in Asia, and the observations made on these
trips have been published in *Journey Without Maps* (1936), *The
Lawless Roads* (1939), and most recently, *In Search of a Character: Two African Journals* (1961).

Something has been said of Greene's early preoccupation with
evil, or what Kenneth Allott and Miriam Farris, his first important
critics, call in their study the "divided mind." Greene himself has
a great deal to say on the subject. In the revealing biographical
sketch, "The Lost Childhood," he gives some indication of his
precocious interest in good and evil. His early reading had been
in Anthony Hope, Rider Haggard, and Marjorie Bowen, stories of
violence and adventure told with gusto and emphasized by melodrama. In the writings of Marjorie Bowen, he says, he learned
that people were not all as good as Allan Quartermain nor as evil
as the witch Gagool. From *The Viper of Milan* he experienced the
fascination of evil, its reality, and found its place in his own life:

As for Visconti, with his beauty, his patience and his genius for evil, I
had watched him pass by many a time in his black Sunday suit smelling
of mothballs. His name was Carter. He exercised terror from a distance
like a snowcloud over the young fields. Goodness had only once found
a perfect incarnation in a human body and never will again, but evil
can always find a home there. Human nature is not black and white
but black and grey. I read all that in *The Viper of Milan* and I looked
round and I saw that it was so.[9]

This preoccupation with evil, with the black and the gray of human life, came upon Greene as a child. His early reading determined the pattern of his writing: "Imitation after imitation of Miss Bowen's magnificent novel went into the exercise books—stories of sixteenth-century Italy or twelfth-century England marked with enormous brutality and a despairing romanticism. It was as if once and for all I had been supplied with a subject." [10] He says:

> . . . religion might later explain it to me in other terms, but the pattern was already there—perfect evil walking the world where perfect good can never walk again, and only the pendulum ensures that after all in the end justice is done. Man is never satisfied, and often I have wished that my hand had not moved further than *King Solomon's Mines*. . . . What is the good of wishing? The books are always there, the moment of crisis waits, and now our children are taking down the future and opening the pages.[11]

The preoccupation with evil was not only discovered in his reading: in *The Lawless Roads* he speaks of his boyhood at his father's school in Berkhamsted. There he lived on the border—between the school dormitories and the family rooms; and the image of the border has become an important one in his work:

> One became aware of God with an intensity—time hung suspended—music lay upon the air. . . . There was no inevitability anywhere . . . faith was almost strong enough to move mountains. . . .
> And so faith came to one—shapelessly, without dogma, a presence above a croquet lawn, something associated with violence, cruelty, evil across the way. One began to believe in heaven because one believed in hell, but for a long while it was hell only one could picture with a certain intimacy—the pitchpine partitions in dormitories where everybody was never quiet at the same time: lavatories without locks: "There, by reason of the great number of the damned, the prisoners are heaped together in their awful prison . . .": walks in pairs up the metroland roads, no solitude anywhere, at any time. The Anglican church could not supply the same intimate symbols for heaven: only a big brass eagle, an organ voluntary, "Lord dismiss us with thy blessing," the quiet croquet lawn where one had no business, the rabbit and the distant music.
> Those were the primary symbols: life later altered them. . . . The Mother of God took the place of the brass eagle: one began to have a

dim conception of the appalling mysteries of love moving through a ravaged world—the Curé d'Ars admitting to his mind all the impurity of a province: Péguy challenging God in the cause of the damned. It remained something one associated with misery, violence, evil, 'all the torments and agonies,' Rilke wrote, 'wrought on scaffolds, in torture chambers, mad-houses, operating theatres, underneath vaults of bridges in late autumn. . . .' [12]

Greene has written further about this period of his life in "The Revolver in the Corner Cupboard." Here he describes his psycho-analysis in London, "perhaps the happiest months in my life," and the boredom that followed upon his correctly "oriented" and "extrovert" interest in life.[13] His early obsessions with evil, with violence and brutality, and with the unhappy found expression in the people of his novels. He could find no meaning in the Anglican Church; he wanted an answer to suffering and misery. This he found in the Catholic Church. The orientation became complete when he met and married Vivien Dayrell-Browning, a Roman Catholic.

The pattern of violence, then, the keynote to much of Greene's work, was set by his early reading. His precocious awareness of good and evil indicated to him his own place in the moral dilemma. His conversion to Roman Catholicism seems to have been a logical step in an intellectual development; in the forms of the Roman Catholic Church he found a measure of an answer to the problems that had vexed him as a child. The Catholic Church offered a reason for suffering and misery, for crime and brutality; it offered the hint of an explanation as to why a fifteen-year-old girl and twenty-year-old boy were found headless on a railway-line, why Irish servant girls met their lovers in ditches, and why the professional prostitute tried to keep the circulation going under her blue and powdered skin.

Greene's Roman Catholicism has given rise to a great deal of critical commentary. Converted to Catholicism at twenty-two, he has remained staunch in his religious convictions—although rumors to the contrary have filtered through the press from time to time. It has been said, and as Miss Knott stated, that the convert to Catholicism takes his religion much more seriously than one born into it. But in his more recent work Greene has demonstrated his ability to use (with artistry and ease) his faith as background. After defining his beliefs in *The Power and the Glory,* he went on to make use of religion without fear of commentary from the critics who found his work "tainted" by "heresies."

The fact is, and it cannot be repeated too often, that Greene is a novelist first and last, not a theologian. His preoccupation is chiefly with the fall of man and with the possibility of redemption. So convincingly does he describe the human dilemma that his readers must comment on his people as though they were living beings. In just such a manner critics have diagnosed for centuries the madness of Hamlet. And Major Scobie's "immortality" is assured partly because of the confusion among Greene's readers concerning his suicide and his redemption, confusion that has arisen chiefly because Scobie's predicament is human and tragic. Indeed, there is implicit in Greene's novels a tendency toward myth; and his characters incontestably assume mythological proportions.

CHAPTER 3

The Entertaining Mr. Greene

WHEN *Brighton Rock* first appeared in 1938, it was listed in the Greene bibliography first as a novel, then as an entertainment. Subsequently the book was reassessed by its author and published as a "novel." Before the publication of *Brighton Rock*, Greene had written a series of slick and exciting stories that had been labeled "novels" and "entertainments" alike. *Brighton Rock* made a dividing point, and the characteristics that distinguish the two "genres" became more readily apparent as other books appeared.

The Man Within, a novel, portrayed Greene's interest in the divided self. The epigraph from Sir Thomas Browne, "There's another man within me that's angry with me," indicated his preoccupation with the problems of good and evil. In this novel Greene followed his hero, Andrews, from his boys' school onto a smuggling vessel where his father had been respected because of his strength and courage, and into a betrayal of Carlyon, his friend, the leader of the smugglers. In a foggy wood, reminiscent of Dante in the *Inferno,* the boy had come upon goodness —Elizabeth, the girl, keeping watch over the corpse of her stepfather who had been killed by the smugglers. At the end of the novel Andrews had been forced to commit suicide not only for having betrayed the smugglers and the girl but also for having betrayed the man within. From this surprisingly excellent novel, the reader became aware of Greene's concern with good and evil, with the black and the gray of human life.

It was not until the publication of *Brighton Rock,* however, that this concern with the nature of good and evil found a frame of reference that is specifically religious. What had been before *Brighton Rock* a deeply felt religious outlook became with this novel the frame of reference within which the action developed.

The novels before *Brighton Rock* had been "secular" in their outlook, those after were "religious," for it was Greene's Roman Catholicism that gave coherence and meaning to the narratives. And Greene's readers and fans alike will concede the fact that the "novels" afford a great deal of material that is at the very least beguilingly controversial.

But what of the entertainments? Much critical attention has been devoted to Greene, the Manichaean; Greene, the theologian; Greene, the Jansenist; Greene, the Existentialist; Greene, the Quietist—and the list could be stretched on and on—but little attention has been given to the nature and quality of the entertainments. Certainly they are thrillers; they lend themselves easily and brilliantly to the idioms of the motion picture, as Greene's list of credits will testify; and they make money for him. Furthermore, a great many of Greene's fans aver that the best of Greene is to be discovered in the entertainments; in them he is intent on telling a good story, on keeping his readers in suspense, and on making the action which is, more often than not, a melodramatic chase, as original and exciting and breathtaking as possible. That Greene is a consummate storyteller and that he knows how to maintain that elusive factor called suspense make him a detective story writer of the highest caliber, the equal of Raymond Chandler, Agatha Christie, Georges Simenon, and S. S. Van Dyne, to name a few masters of the genre. An investigation of the nature of the entertainments will reveal the craftsmanship of Greene's techniques and also point out how, very often, the entertainments are preliminary studies for the more elaborate novels that follow them.

In the Preface to the Viking edition of *The Third Man*, perhaps Greene's most popular entertainment because of its brilliant translation into a motion picture under the direction of Sir Carol Reed, Greene refers to the happy ending that characterizes the thriller type. But whether or not Greene's endings are happy in the conventional sense is a matter for satiric comment, for the endings of his entertainments are often as pessimistic and gloomy as those of his novels. There is one thing, however, that does specifically set the entertainments apart from the novels: the serious preoccupation with religious and ethical problems that the novels pose. The entertainments may indicate the problems, but these are second to the plot, action, and melodrama that distinguish the thriller type. Evelyn Waugh, a Catholic writer of Greene's own stature, distinguishes between the novels and the entertainments in this way: ". . . the 'novels' have been baptized, held deep in under the waters of life. The author has said: 'These characters are not my creation but God's. They have an eternal destiny. They are not merely playing a part for the reader's amusement. They are souls whom Christ died to save.'" [1]

In the novels, except for *The Quiet American*, Greene creates an experience of life in which the religion of the chief actors is Roman Catholicism; in the entertainments, however, religion seems to become superstition or, as is the case with Raven, the hero of *A Gun for Sale* (1936), a sense of loss, of injustice, a feeling of inadequacy, life without justice or pity. In the novels, Greene expends more time and energy on the characterization, and his people react as human beings to the conditions in which they find themselves; in the entertainments, the conditions are more often than not contrived, and causality plays an all important part in the unraveling of the action.

It is, to be sure, interesting to speculate as to the possible theological interpretations of the actions of certain characters in certain novels. But it is essential to remember that these characters—Scobie, Sarah Miles, and the whiskey priest—exist as people in a given experience of life. And if Greene feels that, by portraying men in tragic circumstances, and rubbing the side of his religion long and often enough, he becomes an indispensable opposition in the bringing out of the truth, more power to him. He says, "For to render the highest justice to corruption, you have to be conscious all the time within yourself of treachery to something valuable." [2] If the novelist, who happens to be a Catholic, does not flirt with heresy—as Greene's critics say he often does—he will not be able to understand the attraction of goodness. If he glorifies good by refusing to recognize the fascination of evil, if he desires only to attest the validity of his religion, he becomes, as Greene himself has said, "a philosopher or religious teacher of the second rank." [3] Certainly Greene is neither!

Greene is a writer with a profound sense of evil in the world; and any reader of the essays included in *The Lost Childhood* knows that he had this sense long before his conversion to Roman Catholicism. His novels deal primarily with the fall of man; his entertainments deal with man, perhaps fallen, perhaps not—at any rate, with man in his relationship to other men, not to God. "'Do you believe in God?'" Raven asks Anne Crowder in *A Gun for Sale*. "'I don't know,'" she says. "'Sometimes maybe. It's a habit, praying. It doesn't do any harm. It's like crossing your fingers when you walk under a ladder. We need any luck that's going.'" [4]

Although there is the religious sense present in the entertainments, one might even say that religion and superstition are accounted as one. There is not in them that profound religious conviction that inspires Major Scobie to suicide in *The Heart of the Matter* and the whiskey priest to sainthood in *The Power and the Glory*. Greene's novels, although they make use of the properties of Roman Catholicism, do not attempt to throw light on the teachings of that Church. What Greene is concerned with is the possibility of salvation within the tablets of the law of that Church. And in allowing for personal salvation, Greene allows for heroism; he does this by creating his experiences of life in those uncharted theological regions where the boundaries are blurred.

In *Brighton Rock*, the frame of reference within which the narrative develops is that of the hero's Roman Catholicism. The novel is in the tradition of the detective story, and in it Greene used the same conventions as in the entertainments *Stamboul Train* and *A Gun for Sale*. In these thrillers Greene drew heavily on the atmosphere and symbols of Eliot's *The Waste Land*, and the sense of degeneracy and futility of the poem pervades them. Both books have a "happy" ending, provided the reader accepts Greene's peculiar conviction concerning the nature of the thriller, as mentioned above.

I Stamboul Train

In *Stamboul Train,* Greene used a speeding train as locale for the melodrama that traced Carleton Myatt, a merchant of currants, and Coral Musker, a pitiful chorus girl, through an intrigue that involved murder and a Balkan uprising. In this book Greene sketched the bare outlines of the theme of pity he was to use with such masterful effect in the entertainment, *The Ministry of Fear* (1943) and the novel *The Heart of the Matter* (1948). As film critic for the *Spectator* he had learned a great deal concerning the technique of the cinema, the importance of melodrama, and the necessity of brisk and suspenseful action. Adapting the devices of the Hitchcock movie camera to the needs of the thriller, and perhaps borrowing a little from the Hitchcock classic motion picture *The Lady Vanishes,* Greene used the train with great skill: the halts and stops, the melodramatic chase in Subotica, the inquisitive newspaperwoman, the very lurch and speed of the train —all were contained within a narrative that kept pace with the engine itself. Using the moving-picture camera technique, he moved from point to point on the speeding train, developing his theme and characters on the way, emphasizing the melodrama, and defining his craft.

Myatt's gratitude to Coral, once she had given herself to him, had led him to promise her an apartment of her own in Constantinople; and he had felt responsible for her safety after she had unintentionally involved herself with Dr. Czinner, the revolutionist. He had attempted to rescue her but had successfully pushed his pity aside when the task proved too much for him. As a result of his betrayal, Coral had fallen into the arms of Mabel Warren, the newspaperwoman; and Janet Pardoe, Mabel's friend, into his, Greene thus completing a figure eight pattern to lend unity to the action of the novel. The motif of the chase, the theme of betrayal, the corruption of innocence were all balanced and contained within the entertainment; but the religious sense was there by implication only. The prevailing temper of the book is, therefore, secular.

II A Gun for Sale

A Gun for Sale and *The Ministry of Fear* better illustrate the difference that the religious theme makes in the novels in which it explicitly appears. *A Gun for Sale* is a thriller, fast-paced, tightly organized, economical, and exciting. Again Greene demonstrated his dexterity in handling suspense while adapting the devices of the Hitchcock camera to his materials. Like *Stamboul Train, A Gun for Sale* contains many of the devices of the mystery story: the chase, the confession, the betrayal.

The hero of the novel, James Raven, is, in the Conradian tradition, an anti-hero;[5] he is the protagonist, but he is bitter, antisocial, and desperate—all that the traditional hero is not. Opposing Raven is a strong and determined and unimaginative detective, Mather, who is in love with Anne Crowder, who, like

Coral Musker of *Stamboul Train,* is a chorus girl in second- and third-rate provincial companies. Raven has many things in common with Pinkie Brown, the chief character of *Brighton Rock*—the same sordid background, the squalor of Paradise Place and Nelson Place, the evil that comes with poverty. Both Raven and Pinkie bear the signs of their environment: Raven, his hairlip, Pinkie, his aversion to sex. But Pinkie is a Roman Catholic, Raven is not.

A Gun for Sale is a preliminary study for *Brighton Rock.* The similarity between the two heroes is explicitly made in the mutual relationship they bear to the racetrack protection rackets. The murder of Kite, the leader of Pinkie's gang, is especially recounted by Raven: " 'I was doing the races then. Kite had a rival gang. There wasn't anything else to do. He tried to bump my boss off the course. . . . I cut his throat and the others held him till we were all through the barrier in a bunch' " (176). And it is revenge for Kite's murder that forms the *raison d'être* of *Brighton Rock.*

The action of *A Gun for Sale* moves against the Christmas season—against the cheap religious images, "the plaster mother and child, the wise men and the shepherds"—and against the betrayal of Christ by Judas. Raven makes an association with himself and the holy family for whom there had been no room at the inn. He is angered by the fact that the myth of the birth of Christ is perpetuated by a godless nation:

Love, Charity, Patience, Humility . . . he knew all about those virtues; he'd seen what they were worth. They twisted everything: even the story in there, it was historical, it had happened, but they twisted it to their own purposes. They made him a god because they could feel fine about it all, they didn't have to consider themselves responsible for the raw deal they'd given him. He'd consented, hadn't he? That was the argument, because he could have called down "a legion of angels" if he'd wanted to escape hanging there. On your life he could, he thought with bitter lack of faith. . . .   (122)

The similarity between Pinkie Brown and James Raven is their common betrayal by society and the destruction of their innocence. Raven had seen his mother cut her throat, and Pinkie had witnessed his parents' Saturday night ritual of sex. Although both the entertainment and novel use conventional religious symbolism, in *A Gun for Sale* the symbolism is subordinated to the activity of the novel while in *Brighton Rock* it gives emphasis to the theme and helps push the action into the dimension of religious allegory.

A Gun for Sale also moves against a background of political intrigue. Hired by a fat man, Cholmondeley, to murder an important and humanitarian minister of a small European nation, thus to incite enmity between England and that nation and insure the Midland Steel empire of Cholmondeley's employer, Sir Marcus, Raven is betrayed by both Cholmondeley and Sir Marcus. The theme of flight and pursuit dominates the structure of the novel as Raven attempts to identify his betrayers. Mather, the detective engaged to marry Anne Crowder, follows the trail Raven leaves with his counterfeit money, but he does not know that Raven is the murderer whose deed is exciting the country to war. Anne Crowder, as had her predecessor Coral Musker, becomes unintentionally involved in the action; her pity for Raven leads her first to befriend him, then to help him escape the police so he might destroy Cholmondeley and Sir Marcus if necessary and, as she thinks, prevent war.

It is through Anne Crowder that the theme of betrayal finds its most important development in the novel. The other betrayals do not discomfit Raven, since he trusts no one. His education has taught him to put his faith in no one, particularly in a woman. He cannot understand why Anne befriends him, and he instinctively mistrusts her. Anne herself is willing to take Raven as she finds him until she learns that he is the murderer of the old minister who had dedicated his energies to the prevention of war; and, when she and Raven part, she does not hesitate to betray him to Mather. Willing to befriend him as one of the oppressed, a champion of the poor, she rejects him when she sees him as a betrayer of his class. Raven dies in the knowledge of her treachery, and he associates his betrayal with that of Christ by the Jews. He thinks of the crèche he had seen on arriving in Nottwich. Anne had said to him, "'I'm your friend. You can trust me!'" (237). But she had betrayed him.

Within the symbolic structure of the entertainment, Raven is a scapegoat; the sins of the world are loaded onto his shoulders, a fact he is resentfully aware of. But for all its religious implications, the book is predominantly secular in its outlook. With Raven, however, Greene comes near to the religious intensity that informs the novels beginning with *Brighton Rock*. Betrayed by Anne and the world, Raven reaches out for a God he doesn't believe in. Pinkie, his successor, believes in that same God; but he has rejected Him. Allott and Farris say of Greene's world, "Where there is faith, in Greene, there is the profounder sense of evil and more helpless degeneration." [6] In *A Gun for Sale*, the unforgettable Acky, the unfrocked priest who finds some consolation for his betrayal in the genuine affection which he shares with his grotesque wife, exists as an aspect of evil rather than an exponent of it. Acky's marriage to the ancient procuress is the union of lust and insanity; thus the religious note is held in abeyance.

In their attitude to God, both Anne Crowder and Raven are near to Ida Arnold of *Brighton Rock;* their religion has degenerated into superstition. Anne crosses her fingers when walking under a ladder because she needs any luck that's going, and Ida Arnold consults her ouija board to secure the sanction she needs to avenge Fred Hale's murder. The implied religious note of *A Gun for Sale*—Raven's likening himself to Christ, the "little bastard" betrayed by Judas—becomes in *Brighton Rock* the frame of reference that informs its structure and makes it a consistent allegory on the subject of good and evil, as allegorized in the boy Pinkie and the girl Rose.

The subject matter of *Brighton Rock* is presented in the same melodramatic convention as before; the confrontations and the coincidences still form a portion of the structure. But the chase, the confession, the betrayal, all the devices are subjected to the dominating religious motif, and it becomes an important consideration to understand why damnation is inevitable for Pinkie Brown. *Brighton Rock* is a consistent allegory on the subject of good and evil, the religious framework allowing for the allegorical interpretations. The use of the sensational and the melodramatic permits Greene to present his theme in terms compatible with his religious thesis. The detective story framework sustains and is sustained by the allegory.

Greene makes brilliant use of the images of nature in order to define good and evil in the phenomenal world. The background of Brighton and the sea at once lend the note of reality and form the symbolic background for the allegory; the sea is as real as it is symbolic of continuity. The amusement areas where all is flash and glitter, artifice and tinsel, love songs and rock candy afford an admirable contrast of color for the stark drama of black and white played out against them. The storm in which Pinkie dies emphasizes the spiritual turmoil of the drama, but it does not purge. It exerts its peculiar influence on the reader who agrees with the priest, Greene's spokesman, that the mercy of God is "appalling" to contemplate.

The technique of the cinema camera prepares for the climaxes as Greene moves from scenes of color to scenes of unrelieved drabness, from scenes of purposeless activity to scenes of tense inactivity—Pinkie on the bed amid the remains of his sausage roll, Pinkie looking at the woman who is saved, Ida at the race track. The cinema technique allows the reader to follow the chase, to understand the panic, to savor the suspense.

The conception of *Brighton Rock* is a brilliant one—Graham Greene at his melodramatic best. Following upon *A Gun for Sale,* it demonstrates to what an extent the religious note animates the narrative. And yet both books are very much alike. The fact that *Brighton Rock* makes use of specific religious subject matter distinguishes it from the entertainment and makes it a novel—according to the definition that has been cited.

III   The Confidential Agent

The Confidential Agent, published in 1939, an entertainment, is secular in its outlook in the same sense as *Stamboul Train* and *A Gun for Sale;* and it exhibits the same characteristics—the chase, the revenge, the motif of flight and pursuit. Greene's hero is a middle-aged scholar sent by his government to negotiate a contract with the British mine owners for badly needed coal. He is balked by counteragents and in the end defeated by them. But though he does not secure the coal his country needs, he has the satisfaction of knowing that the enemy will not have it either.

In the characterization of D., the hero, Greene enlarges on the theme of pity which he had lightly sketched in both preceding entertainments. Myatt's concern for Coral and Anne's for Raven had been briefly outlined but had been left undeveloped in order not to intrude on the action of the stories. In *The Confidential Agent,* D. is represented as an elderly scholar who had at one time discovered an important manuscript of *The Song of Roland.* The war, which seems to parallel the war in Spain, had cut short his literary activities and forced him to devote himself to his political party. He is alone, and the death of his wife at the hands of Fascists has paralyzed his feelings. He has nothing to hold on to, not even belief in God. And he cannot be certain of the integrity of the cause for which he fights. "It's no good taking a moral line—my people commit atrocities like the others," he says to Rose Cullen.[7] Like Raven and Anne and Ida Arnold, D. is unable to trust to the God of tradition; and again it is this secular outlook that distinguishes the world of the entertainment.

Although he thinks he is past all feeling, D. is touched by the mute appeal of the child, Else, and by the unhappiness of the girl, Rose Cullen, the daughter of Lord Benditch, D.'s contact for the coal. He finds it impossible to feel love since the death of his wife; but he can feel pity—and pity, according to Greene, can be a corrosive emotion. D.'s pity leads him, eventually, to a "happy" ending; he goes off at the novel's end with Rose.

D. is aware of the evil in the world, but he is passive in the face of it until Else is murdered by the manageress of the hotel in which he lives. (D. had entrusted his identity papers to the child, and she is killed because she remains faithful to the trust.) Once D.'s humanity is aroused by the brutality and senselessness of the murder, he is no longer the pursued but the pursuer. And like Ida Arnold, he can indulge in the luxury of revenge: ". . . If you believed in God, you could also believe that it [the body of Else] had been saved from much misery and had a finer future. You could leave punishment then to God. . . . But he hadn't that particular faith. Unless people received their deserts the world to him was chaos: he was faced with despair." (119)

D. can indulge in the chase to satisfy his sense of outraged humanity; and as long as he adheres to the world's dictum regarding right and wrong, he can allow himself the luxury of revenge, an eye for an eye, a tooth for a tooth. There is no God, so vengeance is D.'s. But in the "religious" novels the issues are much more complex since Greene is concerned in them with the more comprehensive problem of good and evil; right and wrong become aspects of the universal dilemma. The secular attitude is, of course, present in all the novels; but in the entertainments it is the point of view through which Greene develops his characters and his action. And yet by eliminating the religious point of view, Greene does not minimize the religious sense. Ultimately, in all his writings—entertainments, novels, stories, plays—the final point of reference is God.

The Confidential Agent is not so successful an entertainment as *Stamboul Train,* nor does it demonstrate the conciseness and economy of *A Gun for Sale.* And its ending seems somewhat arranged, even considering the melodramatic contrivances of the plot. Greene allows D. to escape the web of evidence that has connected him with the murder of Else, the death of K., the political intrigue in which the government is involved—and all this is done to bring about the "happy" ending which, as Greene wryly implies in the Preface to *The Third Man,* is one of the distinguishing features of the thriller. D. is rewarded for a humanity which nothing has been able to destroy in him—nothing had been able to dry up the pity which responds to the pressure of Else's appeal. The typical Greene child, precocious and sad beyond her years, Else recognizes in D. a largeness of spirit, and her appreciation of his kindness leads to her sacrifice. Her faith engenders in D. a feeling of responsibility, as had Coral's in Myatt.

IV   The Ministry of Fear

The Confidential Agent was followed by *The Lawless Roads,* a travel book in 1939 and by *The Power and the Glory,* a novel, in 1940. *The Ministry of Fear,* an entertainment, appeared in 1943, and it stands in relation to *The Heart of the Matter* much as *A Gun for Sale* does to *Brighton Rock.* And like Greene's other entertainments, it is fast-paced, melodramatic, exciting—perhaps his best. It depends on coincidence for much of its action; and, unlike *Stamboul Train* and *A Gun for Sale,* it makes use of an actual war for its *mise en scène:* London at the height of the blitz. In this novel Greene exploits the theme of pity, which he uses to great advantage in *The Heart of the Matter.* In *The Ministry of Fear* pity emerges as the central motif; and it is around the pity in Arthur Rowe, the hero, that much of the action turns.

In *The Ministry of Fear,* pity is shown to be a corrosive sentiment which, if allowed to develop disproportionately, creates in its advocate a sense of responsibility which at once sets him apart from his fellow beings and, paradoxically, causes him to love them the more for being apart. The overwhelming sentiment of pity makes Arthur Rowe capable of bearing pain but equally incapable of causing hurt to others. He becomes involved in the activities of a fifth-column organization operating in bomb-torn London, an organization which uses as its front a charity, Comforts for Mothers of the Free Nations Fund. Unwittingly and unwillingly Rowe becomes the spokesman of humanity and the opponent of the cult of power, the same cult to which the lieutenant subscribes in *The Power and the Glory*.

The entertainment is divided into four parts: The first deals with Rowe, the man who killed his wife out of pity. It sets the stage for the action and portrays the trapping incident, the fête; ironically, in the cake that Rowe wins, the spy ring has placed the microfilm of secret naval plans. The second section deals with the happy man, the Rowe who has lost the memory of his past, the sense of pity that has propelled him since adolescence. The third begins his reorientation—Rowe slowly discovers what his beliefs and convictions are, and, since he is not reacquainted with the sense of responsibility that characterized him before, he is still happy. In the fourth and last section, called "The Whole Man," Rowe returns to Anna Hilfe, the woman who loves him, in complete knowledge of his past and her attempts to safeguard him from that knowledge. To portray these stages, Greene is forced to present his action chiefly from Rowe's point of view in order to arouse and maintain the suspense factor so important to the entertainments. Willi Hilfe, the representative of the cult of power, is developed from the "outside."

In *The Power and the Glory*, Greene's portrayal of the lieutenant develops the inner motives of the power addict, particularly his antagonism to the Roman Catholic Church and all it represents to the power state. Greene gives expression to these views in the dramatic debates with the whiskey priest. The religion of power to which the lieutenant aspires is shown to be a thing of particular beauty. Violence and brutality, in the lieutenant's philosophy, are tools necessary to secure the operation of a "religion" which offers as its sacraments food, shelter, education. In *The Ministry of Fear*, however, Willi Hilfe is minimally characterized, and the philosophy that animates his actions is left undeveloped. For purposes of the plot and the surprise ending, Willi emerges at the entertainment's end as Rowe's antagonist. The reader discovers along with Rowe that Willi had attempted to murder his sister Anna as well as Rowe, and that he had arranged for the murder of Jones, the inept detective. The reader is asked to accept the personification of evil as it is; and he does. The action develops with speed and ingenuity; such melodramatic contrivances as a séance, a sanitarium, a "Roman death" in a fashionable tailor shop, and a sensational suicide in a lavatory counterpointing the suspense generated by falling bombs, the constant threat of death from the enemy—indeed the puzzle itself—all excuse the many irregularities of characterization.

Pity is, however, the dominant theme of the book. Arthur Rowe had killed his wife because he could not bear to have her suffer from an incurable disease. He cannot be certain whether he killed her to free himself of her pain or to relieve her of it. The courts had found him not guilty and had released him to a life of haunted responsibility. He stumbles upon a fair, drawn to it "like innocence." He is reminded of vicarage gardens and of girls in cool summer frocks; he is reminded of security. He remembers a Charlotte M. Yonge book, *The Little Duke*, and Greene ingeniously uses snatches of it as epigraphs to set the mood of his chapters. The fair allows Rowe to set aside temporarily the misfortunes of twenty years that have taught him, a man "with a too sensitive mouth," to love too well: "People could always get things out of him by wanting them enough: it broke his precarious calm to feel that people suffered. Then he would do anything for them. Anything." [8] The pity that Rowe feels for ugliness and misfortune makes him a bondsman of his emotion. At a cry of unhappiness or alarm he is ready to commit himself to any course of action. He has a sense of God, but it is undefined. As a boy he had been taught to believe, but somehow he had lost his childhood faith, preferring to depend on his own feelings for assurance of love. But his own feelings exaggerate the sense of pity and make of him a victim to those who appeal to him.

The religious sense is, perhaps, more explicitly portrayed in *The Ministry of Fear* than in Greene's other entertainments: for Rowe's sense of the loss of innocence is, inexplicably to him, somehow a sense of the loss of God:

Listening Rowe thought, as he so often did, that you couldn't take such an odd world seriously; though all the time he did, in fact, take it with a mortal seriousness. The grand names stood permanently like statues in his mind: names like Justice and Retribution. . . . But of course if you believed in God—and the Devil—the thing wasn't quite so comic. Because the devil—and God too—had always used comic people, futile people, little suburban natures and the maimed and warped to serve his purposes. When God used them you talked emptily of Nobility, and when the devil used them of Wickedness, but the material was only dull shabby human mediocrity in either case. (30-31)

This passage indicates strongly why Greene peoples his universe with the seedy, the unhappy, with "dull shabby human mediocrity."

With the betrayal of childhood innocence comes the knowledge of the phenomenal world, and the Wordsworthian theme—"the clouds of glory"—is developed. Aware only of "simplicities," a child does not understand the sense of pity which occasionally overtakes him, as it had overtaken the boy Rowe when he had killed the rat to keep it from suffering, one of his earliest memories. The child, in Wordsworthian idiom, becomes father of the man. For Rowe the man is Arthur the boy; the boy had killed the rat, the man his wife. With his loss of innocence had come the realization that humanity cannot be loved in the abstract; only men and women can be loved. And this is exactly the lesson that the whiskey priest learns in *The Power and the Glory*.

The Arcadian interlude in the sanitarium after Rowe's memory has been lost, becomes for him a period of reorientation into the world. He rediscovers the idyl of his childhood, but he also discovers the necessity of love—its inevitability. If one loves men and women, Rowe discovers, then it becomes necessary to love and hate as they do, "and if that were the end of everything suffer damnation with them" (155). Rowe's love for Anna Hilfe, his betrayer's sister, leads him inevitably toward suffering, loss, and despair. The sense of pity finds its man at the entertainment's end, and it is still the corrosive influence it had always been. The commentary on the theme is made by Prentice, the man from Scotland Yard: " 'Pity is a terrible thing. People talk about the passion of love. Pity is the worst passion of all: we don't outlive it like sex' " (206).

Rowe's passionate pity is indeed a form of egotism, for it insists that the individual assume responsibility for his fellow men without consulting God. It implies a lack of trust and of faith, and in *The Ministry of Fear* this point is left unexplored, since the book exhibits the characteristics of the entertainments. In *The Heart of the Matter*, this theme becomes more explicit. Both Rowe's and

Scobie's responsibility for and concern with unhappiness characterize them to such an extent that they become, paradoxically, humble men, bondsmen to those they love. The parallel drawn with Christ is implicit. Major Scobie, like Arthur Rowe, is defined by his pity; but as a Roman Catholic, he is aware of God in the world. And it is his religious belief that distinguishes *The Heart of the Matter* from *The Ministry of Fear:* What in the entertainment is a religious sense becomes in the novel a religious theme.

V   The Third Man

Greene's next entertainment, *The Third Man,* was written in 1950 for the motion pictures. In the Preface to the Viking edition, Greene explains that, before he could write a script for Sir Alexander Korda and Sir Carol Reed, he had first of all to develop the line of his story's action. *The Third Man,* never intended for publication, is the result. Greene admits that the motion picture is better than the story "because it is in this case the finished state of the story," an admission not wholly accurate.[9]

The Third Man is interesting in that it contains in brief many of Greene's favorite themes. The entertainment concerns the penicillin racket in Vienna immediately after World War II. Harry Lime, the black marketeer, calls his friend Rollo Martins, a writer of western adventure stories, to describe the occupation of the city; but Rollo arrives in time for Harry's funeral. He suspects that Harry has been murdered, and he refuses to accept the police inspector's explanation that Lime was implicated in the rackets. Investigating for himself, Martins meets Harry's friends and Anna Schmidt, his mistress. He learns from Harry's landlord that three men had carried the body to the pavement on the night that Harry had been run over by a truck, but the police can account for only two. The action of the entertainment depends on Rollo's finding the third man.

Vienna under the four-power occupation allows Greene to develop many of *The Waste Land* images. The city itself is reminiscent of Eliot's Unreal City, and the title of the book owes as much to Eliot as it does to the Bible:

> *Who is the third who walks always beside you?*
> *When I count, there are only you and I together*
> *But when I look ahead up the white road*

There is always another one walking beside you
Gliding wrapt in a brown mantle, hooded
I do not know whether a man or a woman
—But who is that on the other side of you? [10]

The Biblical reference, in the twenty-fifth chapter of Luke, is, of course, to the travelers to Emmaus. They are accompanied on their journey by a third man, and that man is Christ. In *The Third Man,* that shadowy figure is ostensibly Harry Lime; symbolically it is Christ who accompanies Rollo Martins in his search. Keeping one step ahead of the police, Lime had falsified his death. So Martins, looking for Harry's murderer, looks for Harry. In his search he discovers that the man "he has hero-worshipped now for twenty-five years, since the first meeting in a grim school corridor with a cracked bell ringing for prayers," is, in reality, a child who has somewhere, somehow, replaced the innocence of childhood with the evil of maturity.

The search motif in *The Third Man* parallels that in Greene's other works—it is jointly a search of recognition and a search for meaning. Once he realizes that Lime by selling adulterated penicillin causes more suffering to those who already suffer, Rollo becomes the aggressor. The third man whom he seeks in reality accompanies him, for he is Rollo's sense of justice, his faith. The religious implications of the entertainment are subdued, held in check by the more important demands of the action and the melodrama. But they appear nevertheless. Both Harry and Rollo are Catholics, although they wear their religion with greater nonchalance than do other of Greene's characters. Their faith becomes important in the final action of the story, for Rollo's pity overwhelms his sense of duty, and he kills Harry rather than allow him to endure pain.

Within the pattern of the entertainment Lime is the exponent of the cult of power. In dealing in black-market goods, Harry not only puts himself above the law but presumes to judge individual humanity. He says to Rollo: " 'It's the fashion. In these days, old man, nobody thinks in terms of human beings. Governments don't, so why should we? They talk of the people and the proletariat, and I talk of mugs. It's the same thing. They have their five-year plans and so have I' " (139).

It would be unfair to condemn *The Third Man* as an inferior production. It is simple, economical, austere. If, as an entertainment, it does not measure up to the standards of Greene's earlier works, it must be remembered that the final version of the story is, as Greene says, the motion picture. And as a motion picture *The Third Man* was outstanding. The city of Vienna, its bombed-out houses, its sewers "a cavernous land of waterfalls and rushing rivers, where tides ebb and flow as in the world above" (148), indeed the region of the dead, formed the most suitable background for the portrayal of the Greene themes. The black and white photography and the strange music of the zither combined to make a strikingly excellent entertainment. The cogency of the Greene themes found commensurate exposition in the visual technique of the camera. And one can only say that "the finished state of the story" is as successful as any other Greene entertainment.

VI   Loser Takes All

The End of the Affair, a novel published in 1951, following *The Third Man,* demonstrates Greene's growing concern with the craft of fiction. The melodramatic contrivances of *Brighton Rock* and the entertainments and the dramatic technique of *The Power and the Glory* and *The Heart of the Matter* are replaced by devices more consistent within the forms of the modern novel: the use of a narrator, the stream-of-consciousness technique, the flashback, the diary to explain motivation, the interior reverie, and the spiritual debate—all are used with extreme discretion as Greene tells his story about Sarah Miles, a woman who finds God and, possibly, sainthood. *The End of the Affair* is perhaps Greene's best constructed novel, although it is not his most successful. It was followed by *The Living Room,* a drama, in 1953, and by *Loser Takes All,* an entertainment, in 1955. Like *The Third Man, Loser Takes All* was originally written for the films, but it is a far cry from the other entertainments.

Slight, easy-going, entertaining, *Loser Takes All* is a story of a Monte Carlo honeymoon. A middle-aged accountant husband, Bertram, and his bride are invited by his employer, the Gom— short for Grand Old Man—to be his guests during their honeymoon. The Gom forgets to show up, and Bertram is forced to invent a system at roulette in order to live while waiting. The system works, and Bertram becomes a comparatively wealthy man.

He then buys some important stocks in his firm from a reluctant stockholder who is temporarily out of funds while trying his own system at the roulette tables. Bertram almost loses his bride, but he chooses to lose the fortune he has won and keep his wife. The Gom finally sails into the harbor in time to tell Bertram how to get back his wife, thus suggesting a God figure.

Loser Takes All is a bright, occasionally witty, but rather inconsequential entertainment; perhaps it is just a long story, lacking as it does the depth and flow of the early entertainments and novels. Nevertheless, it is important in the Greene *oeuvre* because it demonstrates that Greene can be lighthearted and can develop a theme that is primarily comic if he wants. Those expecting the intense gloom and pessimism of the early Greene will be disappointed, for *Loser Takes All* and its successor entertainment, *Our Man in Havana,* are both lighthearted and easygoing. Yet they are excellently done, for Greene is above all a craftsman of distinction.

VII   Our Man in Havana

Very often what the novels lose, the entertainments gain: a sense of movement and space, a feeling of power and imagination. But as often as not the novels gain what the entertainments lack: a deep insight into those dark corners of behavior that Greene loves to uncover, even if uncovering involves questioning the beliefs of his faith. Greene's latest entertainment, *Our Man in Havana,* published in 1958, is a blessed relief from the high and serious tone that pervaded much of his earlier work. *Our Man in Havana* is, among other things, a delightful satire with a serious edge, one of the funniest books to appear in many a day, and a complete change of pace for Greene the artist. And this is significant because the book illustrates again the range of Greene's creative genius; it gives the reader a closer look at his flair for comedy, which remained latent in the early novels and entertainments and which is barely perceptible in a few of the short stories. Greene's sense of irony, so apparent in the overly criticized and perhaps abused *The Quiet American*—the one novel in which Greene uses indirectly rather than specifically a religious subject matter—is apparent here; but it is controlled by the author's appreciation of the tone and intention of his book.

Set in the near future, which appears uncomfortably like the immediate present, *Our Man in Havana* is like the other entertainments: an economical, tightly constructed, exciting satire on the exploits of the British Secret Service abroad. But, unlike the other entertainments, it is amusing, witty; in short, entertaining. Chief agent for Phastcleaner vacuum cleaners, Jim Wormold, whose name is descriptive of his character as are those of other Greene characters, is one of the commercially unsuccessful, a group of people whom Greene dearly loves. Middle-aged, walking with a limp, early deserted by a beautiful wife but blessed with a beautiful daughter whom he has promised to bring up a Roman Catholic although he himself has no formal religion, Wormold finds his position in Havana difficult but not impossible.

His chief difficulty is economic, for his daughter Milly has expensive tastes. She prays to her patron saints and makes novenas for what she wants, and she usually succeeds in getting it since Wormold can deny her nothing. He feels that there is something theologically wrong with her methods, but he is too kindly to remonstrate; and Milly points out to him time on time that he is an "invincibly ignorant" pagan. Wormold solves his financial difficulties by becoming a spy for the British Secret Service; he then invents spies, borrows names from the Country Club registry, and by borrowing for his "spies" and for himself against an expense account manages to secure Milly's future. Eventually Wormold's creations spring unaccountably to life, and he is forced to a reckoning. By fabricating facts and passing them off as secret data, Wormold brings about the deaths of a young aviator and his best friend, Dr. Hasselbacher. His sense of guilt leads him to avenge their deaths; and, luckily for him, he succeeds, without being technically responsible for the death of the counterspy Carter. Deported from Havana and back in London, his exploits now known by his employers, Wormold wonders what is to be done with him, for legally he is not guilty of espionage—all his information had been invented and his one actual attempt at espionage had proved a failure. To his embarrassment the Secret Service presents him with a medal and makes him an instructor in the espionage school, an ironic reward for his bungling.

Anyone looking for deep philosophical and religious meaning in *Our Man in Havana* will be disappointed, for Greene does nothing more in the entertainment than entertain. The satire and the ease with which Greene moves into the field of comedy make

Our Man in Havana significant, and as an entertainment it gains and fails as his previous efforts have gained and failed—it is short in characterization but long in incident and detail. Nevertheless, Greene's criticism of the contemporary political scene is as intelligent as ever it was in such early novels of social commentary as *England Made Me* and *It's a Battlefield*, and it is tinged with that pessimism and melancholy that the Greene reader has come to identify as an important aspect of the Greene universe. He pokes fun at stupid, bureaucratic procedure and—indirectly and rather amusedly—at the heavy-handed irony of some of his earlier efforts. He criticizes the atomic age: Hasselbacher says, " 'We none of us have a great expectation of life nowadays, so why worry? . . . Push a button—pff bang—where are we?' " [11] And again Hasselbacher says, " 'You should dream more, Mr. Wormold. Reality in our century is not something to be faced' " (5). Beatrice, Wormold's secretary says, " 'The world is modelled after the popular magazines nowadays' " (135). So it is no wonder that Wormold models his espionage activities on the comic strip adventures of any number of popular heroes. All we need do is turn on our television sets to see the truth of Greene's observations. Wormold reasons that if one must play a child's game, he might as well play it all the way.

Wiser than a child, however, Wormold remembers that, when he plays games with Milly, she inevitably requires her money back. And, in such seemingly artless comments as these, Greene suggests, haltingly and tentatively, where before he had done so belligerently and dogmatically, the ultimate responsibilities of the individual. It is the epigraph that gives the reader the clue to the characterization: "And the sad man is cock of all his jests." Melancholy, concerned over his daughter's future, Wormold remains true to his only ideal, his feeling for the beautiful child. His secretary, who grows to love him, voices an important aspect of the entertainment's theme when she says, " 'I don't care a damn about men who are loyal to the people who pay them, to organizations. . . . I don't think even my country means that much. There are many countries in our blood—aren't there?—but only one person. Would the world be in the mess it is if we were loyal to love and not to countries?' " (214). Butt of all his own jests, Wormold has learned that simple loyalty to one person is not enough, that ultimately loyalty must be given to an ideal stronger than an individual. If *Our Man in Havana* had been a novel rather than an entertainment, it might perhaps have developed this consideration. And the character of Wormold would have been drawn from within rather than from without. But this criticism is unfair; for the reader must concede that *Our Man in Havana* is exactly what Greene intends it to be—an entertainment that is entertaining.

Ultimately Greene is important for the scope and originality of the novels that have provoked critics and readers alike into philosophical and religious arguments. But, as has already been pointed out, Greene is primarily a creative writer who happens to be a Catholic, not a Catholic writer. The fact that he uses his Church as background for the action of many of his books is incidental to the main appreciation of his artistry. The entertainments are not the thought-provoking documents that the novels are, but they are interesting pieces that throw a good deal of light on the meaning and technique of the major novels. Above all, they are first rate in their genre, books that any writer of thrillers or light fiction would be proud to have written. And they demonstrate, above all, the versatility of the writer—his many parts, to use the Elizabethan expression. No wonder then that Greene is thought by many to be one of the greatest writers of our language and, perhaps, our finest living novelist.

CHAPTER 4

The Early Work

V AGUELY historical in outline, *The Man Within* had dealt with good and evil in the divided character of the young Andrews. The girl Elizabeth had come to symbolize idealism in the world, and the prostitute Lucy the demands of the animal self. The theme of betrayal, for Andrews betrays both Carlyon his friend and Elizabeth, had formulated the design of the novel, and the action had been presented primarily from the point of view of the fleeing boy. After the death of Elizabeth, Andrews had changed from pursued to hunter, thus reversing the motif of flight and pursuit; Andrews' suicide at the novel's end becomes in effect his triumph over the division of his character.

Published in 1934, *It's a Battlefield*, is a departure in both mood and purpose from *The Man Within*, but not in theme—betrayal and responsibility. In order to emphasize the spiritual dilemma of the fleeing boy, Greene had kept the backgrounds of *The Man Within* foggy; *It's a Battlefield* is modern in setting and sociological in intention. In it Greene allows himself great latitude in portraying ironically and, to a certain extent, satirically twentieth-century institutions and attitudes.

It's a Battlefield has as its central metaphor the battlefield. The epigraph describes an actual battle, "each separate gathering of English soldiery . . . fighting its own little battle in happy and advantageous ignorance of the action; nay, even very often in ignorance of the fact that any great conflict was raging." To Greene the battlefield is the world of human affairs in which God figures very little or not at all. Both Lady Caroline Bury and the Assistant Commissioner of Police dream of the millennium, yet both are too realistic to believe it near at hand. The battlefield is also the world of human emotions where betrayal and greatness are found next to each other. This world is depicted in the reactions of the several characters to the imprisonment and impending execution, or reprieve of that execution, of Jim Drover who, in the heat of a Communist rally, had killed a policeman while protecting his wife, Milly. The action of the novel is presented through the points of view of the characters whose lives are directly and indirectly affected by the question of justice to Drover.

First there is the Assistant Commissioner of Police, interested only in facts; in this respect he anticipates the lieutenant of *The Power and the Glory*. The Assistant Commissioner believes that justice, morality, and politics are not his concern in the battlefield; in this respect he differs from the lieutenant. Asked to investigate public reaction to the execution of Drover, the Assistant Commissioner concludes that the execution will in no way affect the popularity of the government in power. Opposed to the Assistant Commissioner, whose very inarticulateness becomes ironically emblematic of his rationalistic attitude, is Lady Caroline Bury, whose interference in the Drover case is prompted as much by humanitarian instincts as by an unwillingness to admit pain and suffering. " 'I'm frightened of pain,' " she says. " 'I've never been able to stand pain.' " [1] Her concern leads her to suggest that the minister who is responsible for Drover might not be above bribery.

Ironically, Lady Caroline and the Assistant Commissioner are the two spectators who are best equipped to see into the real issues underlying Drover's predicament: social injustice and hypocrisy. In the act of making her will as she speaks to the Assistant Commissioner on Drover's behalf, she concludes that she cannot leave her considerable wealth to the state "as it's run at the present" (218). Lady Caroline is sustained by a vague faith, as her friend the Assistant Commissioner is not; ironically, they who represent intelligence and humanitarianism part without warmth.

Those who would be most affected by Drover's execution are his wife and his brother Conrad. Should Drover's death sentence be commuted, he would remain imprisoned for eighteen years. Milly, in love with her husband, would face the impossible task of remaining faithful to him; Conrad, in love with Milly, the impossible task of remaining faithful to both. Again, the triangle relationship that informs the action of many of Greene's pieces determines the complexities of the plot.

Like others of Greene's heroines, Milly demonstrates a certain inept malice; this malice is her defense against the importunities of the world. She is very close to Rose Cullen in *The Confidential Agent:* "Her happiness had always been shot through with touches of malice. Her husband, contented with his job and his pay, had been the Communist; not Milly, contented with nothing but his love, suspicious of the whole world outside. She had never been able to believe that they would be left alone to enjoy each other. Her malice had been a form of defense, an appeal to other people to 'leave us alone' " (70).

She determines that if she gets the widow of the policeman Jim stabbed to sign a petition asking for commutation, she will be doing something useful in her husband's cause. She proves successful, and for a brief hour enjoys the surging emotion of power. But her happiness is cut short by Conrad, Jim's "successful" brother. More out of pity than out of love, he seduces her to shield her from the horrors of life: "He felt no guilt at all; this did not harm his brother, this hopeless attempt to shield her, for she had not even been deceived; she was glad, she was grateful, she was his friend. . . ." (143). The love that was to have ennobled him has in effect been prompted by compassion: "They had been driven to it, and holding her body close to him with painful tenderness, it was hate he chiefly felt, hate of Jim, of a director's nephew, of two men laughing in Piccadilly" (144). Conrad buys a second-hand pistol and sets about tracking the Assistant Commissioner. Ironically, the pistol is loaded with blanks, and Conrad is run down by a car after making an abortive attempt at murder. The motif of flight and pursuit thus unifies the actions of those officially and those personally concerned with the execution of Jim Drover.

On the periphery are Kay Rimmer, Milly's sister; her lover Jules, whose overcautiousness keeps him from finding happiness with Kay; Mr. Surrogate, the dilettante political philosopher, whose Communism is sham and whose opinion, ironically correct, is that Drover's death will do the party more good than a long imprisonment; and Conder, the newspaperman, who, to relieve the bleakness of his celibacy, invents for himself a family circle of wife, six children, and the concomitant annoyances of domestic bliss. Those who know his many poses—a master spy or, at times, a debonair bachelor—pity him; those who believe his fantasies, envy him. The lives of these bystanders are affected by Jim Drover insomuch as they are thrown together as they rally to his cause. They can be compared to the bystanders of *The Power and the Glory* whose lives are changed by the whiskey priest as he moves toward his salvation.

The activities of the battlefield unify the novel's plot. Milly and Conrad pursue the battle in their own ways: Milly secures the signature of the murdered policeman's wife on the petition; Conrad foolishly buys the pistol and attempts to assassinate the Assistant Commissioner. Although Kay resents the fact that her brother-in-law has got into difficulty, she nevertheless enjoys the notoriety that her position gives her with Surrogate, who first introduces Lady Caroline to the problem. Ineffectual Jules enters the lists but simply forgets to do anything at all; and Conder seeks his facts, while his imagination works overtime. The essential conflict, however, is interpreted by the Assistant Commissioner and Lady Caroline, dispassionately by the one, passionately by the other.

The imagery of the novel suggests the prison, while the metaphor of the battlefield suggests the struggle. The actual prison where Jim awaits his fate is described early in the story, its cell blocks full of inmates, some preferred and some not. Kay's factory is described in identical terms; the various parts of the works become cell blocks, some workers are preferred above others, and the girls are satirically named Greta, Marlene, and Kay—devotees of the cult of artificial beauty. Surrogate's pink bedroom is his cell, for he awakens each morning to the scrutiny of his dead wife's eyes in the portrait that hangs beyond his bed; his jailer is his valet, who knows him for the lecherous fraud he is. Conrad's office is still another aspect of the prison; his success has come to him step by step, much to his surprise, and he has disciplined himself to accept each promotion with humility. And finally Milly's home, the basement flat, is a prison since her husband's imprisonment. The metaphor of the battlefield and the image of the prison at the same time lend unity to a marvelously integrated plot and emphasize the sociological implications.

England Made Me, published in 1935, is less sociological in its implications than *It's a Battlefield* but equally somber in mood. The novel deals chiefly with the affinities between twins, Anthony and Kate Farrant, and their responsibility for and to Erik Krogh, a character modeled on Ivar Kreuger, the Swedish industrialist and a self-made man. Again the theme of betrayal is dominant, but to it is closely bonded the theme of fraternal love that borders on incest. By being born a few minutes earlier, Kate stole from her twin brother the initiative one expects in a man. Anthony gathers as his share of their joint birthright the charm that would have served his sister better.

The short story, "The End of the Party," dated 1929 in *Nineteen Stories,* deals with the relationship of identical twins and with the idea that one gains initiative at the other's expense. At the conclusion of "The End of the Party," Francis Morton dies during a game of hide-and-seek when his brother's hand touches his, and Peter inherits his dead brother's fear. In many ways "The End of the Party" looks forward to *England Made Me,* as does the novel fragment "The Other Side of the Border," also included in *Nineteen Stories.* Greene writes in a note to this fragment: "Why did I abandon the book? I think for two main reasons— because another book, *Brighton Rock,* was more insistent to be written, and because I realized that I had already dealt with the main character in a story called *England Made Me.* Hands, I realized, had the same origin as Anthony Farrent [*sic*] in that novel." [2]

Both Hands, the hero of the fragmentary novel, and Anthony Farrant are made of the same material; both are seedy adventurers who lack even enough courage for jail, and both are at once optimistic and diffident about their charm and their ability to see themselves through. Anthony wears his smile "as a leper carried his bell"; as a perpetual warning that he is not to be trusted. Early in the novel he asks Kate to stick to him: " 'Of course,' she said. There was nothing easier to promise. She could not rid herself of him. He was more than her brother; he was the ghost that warned her, look what you have escaped; he was all the experience that she had missed; he was pain, because she had never felt pain except through him; for the same reason he was fear, despair, disgrace. He was everything except success." [3]

The motif of the soured innocence, one that Greene makes capital use of in "The Basement Room" (1935) and in *Brighton Rock,* finds its place within the novel's structure. As children Kate and Anthony had met in a barn; Kate had encouraged Anthony to return to school, and the pattern of his existence had been set

—his deceits, his hopeless infantilism, his calculated interests. Kate thinks: "If I could put back time, if I could twist this ring Krogh gave me and abolish all this place . . . it would be dark now and a wind outside and the smell of manure and he with his cap in his hand, and I'd say: 'Don't go back. Never mind what people say. Don't go back,' and nothing would be the same" (25). Kate had sent Anthony back into the world of conformity and tradition and had made him unfit for the great world of affairs.

The only art that Anthony possesses is that of sharpshooter. At a fair he shoots supremely well and wins for his efforts a vase, which Kate drops and breaks, and a toy tiger. Within the action of the novel, both these items assume symbolical proportions. Francis Kunkel in *The Labyrinthine Ways of Graham Greene* points out the symbolical implications of the tiger, "a symbol of Anthony's evasion of responsibility," but he neglects the ironical, almost whimsical, reference to both William Blake and T. S. Eliot.[4] The tiger is a symbol of Anthony's initiative and virility; he promises it to Kate, but it is destined for Lucia Davidge, Loo. The broken vase, of course, suggests the impossibility of the brother-sister love relationship. Furthermore, the tiger leads the reader to Loo, and in Anthony's meeting with her on the North Bridge another Eliot note is struck and the ending prepared for:

He thought, one could hardly be more wet if one had been fished up from the lake, and because a thought of that kind was apt to weigh like a cold compress too long on his brain, he laughed it away, "I'm a good swimmer." But it was not true. He had always feared the water: he had been flung into a bath to sink or swim by his father when he was six and he had sunk. For years afterwards he dreamed of death by drowning. But he had outwitted whatever providence it was that plotted always to fit a man with the death he most dreaded. (149)

England Made Me is similar in structure to *It's a Battlefield* in its manipulation of point of view, its use of irony, and its handling of the theme of betrayal. The activity of the novel is partly described through Kate's eyes, and the emphasis falls on her possessive love for her brother. She is Krogh's mistress, but her relationship to him is prompted by self-interest and admiration, not by love. Her only agreeable sexual experience with Krogh had been brought on by the stimulus of a visitor who reminded her of Anthony. Anthony's point of view, like Kate's, is controlled by his feeling for his twin. In moments of genuine feeling he admits that he is as bound to her as she is to him. Yet sex is important to him, for it is a large part of love. Love is to Anthony as it is to Ida Arnold, "having a bit of fun"; it is Mabel and Annette and Loo, the hot handclasp in the taxi, the wet mouth, and the tumbled bed.

But Kate's love is for Anthony alone. To have Anthony with her in Stockholm is the full realization of all her plans, what she has plotted and schemed for; yet having Anthony with her is ironically his destruction. Her position as Krogh's mistress is to secure Anthony's future as well as her own; when Krogh asks her to marry, she asks for a settlement for Anthony and herself. To deny Anthony is to deny herself; to deny Krogh seems to her at first a betrayal of the future; and the symbol of this future is the statue in Krogh's lobby, a statue that she admires. Once she realizes that Krogh is not the future but one of "the shipwrecked," to refer to the American title that Greene used to describe the action of the novel, she need no longer dissimulate. But Anthony's betrayal of Krogh is his betrayal of Kate and of himself. Krogh alone is capable of saving himself.

Another part of the action of the novel is described from the point of view of the ruthless and lonely industrialist Erik Krogh. In a scene of hilarious, yet ironic, comic invention—a scene that looks forward to Milly's birthday party in *Our Man in Havana,* the comic involvements of *The Complaisant Lover,* and the comedy of "Beyond the Garden"—Krogh's character is revealed. Anthony's presence and their escape from the Wagnerian opera prompt in Krogh a memory of happier times before the invention of that vague and undefined "cutter" that brought with it wealth, fame, and responsibility. In a moment of calculated generosity, Krogh agrees to give the newspaperman, Professor Hammarstein, the money to produce Shakespeare's *Pericles.*

The action of the novel is further described through the points of view of Minty, the Anglican newspaperman, a remittance man whose life ceased when he left Harrow under a cloud; by Hall, Krogh's hatchet man, who is responsible for Anthony's murder; and by young Andersen, a young and idealistic employee of Krogh's who is somehow involved in a strike that Krogh is attempting to avert. The point of view is supported by Greene's use of the stream-of-consciousness, the technique that he uses best in *The End of the Affair*. A case in point is Kate's reverie in the second section of Part II. She awakens at Krogh's side, thinks of the impending strike, of Anthony and his job with Krogh's, and of the toy tiger, the tiger which weaves its way through the entire activity of the novel. She thinks of her position with Krogh, again of Anthony and of the tiger, and then of Krogh and the only time she desired him, then of her dying father, and again of Anthony. The tiger and the blue vase, broken. Then the tiger burning bright, its sinews of jealousy, of Anthony, of her father. And then the brilliant foreshadowing passage:

> Don't be afraid. Don't hesitate. No cause of fear. No bulls on this exchange. The tiger bright. The forests. Sleep. Our bond. The new redemption. And we rise, we rise. And God Who made the lamb made Whitaker, made Loewenstein. 'But you are lucky,' Hammond said that day in Leather Lane, 'Krogh's safe. Whatever comes or goes people will always everywhere have to buy Krogh's.' The market steady. The Strand, the water and a street between us. Sleep. The new redemption. No bulls, the tiger and the lamb. The bears. The forests. Sleep. The stock is sound. The closing price. We rise.   (82)

The English characters of the novel are contrasted to those of European or Scandinavian extraction; although a great emphasis is put on Krogh's internationalism, Kate, Anthony, Minty and, to a certain extent, the Davidges recognize the advantages and limitations of their British upbringing. Anthony's fate is dictated by the standards of English society which he is unequipped to contend with, although he "puts up a good show." Kate's relationship to Krogh is conditioned by her brother's feeling that one's sister does not ask her lover to find work for her brother. Minty is contented to remember with nostalgia the delights of Harrow, and he treasures nothing more than a letter from "the family."

Both *It's a Battlefield* and *England Made Me* are brilliantly planned and executed novels. The controlling temper of both is secular, although the religious note is tentatively sounded by the toy tiger and the death-by-water references in the latter book. Both novels indicate an enormous growth in both style and plot construction since *The Man Within*, and both look forward to the later and perhaps more provocative novels beginning with *Brighton Rock*.

CHAPTER 5

The Major Novels

I Brighton Rock

MOVING from the world of *Stamboul Train* and *A Gun for Sale* into that of *Brighton Rock* is much like moving from the square of a medieval village into the dim light of the cathedral to contemplate God under the storied capitals where the demons and angels battle for the soul of man. Indeed, the morality aspect of the novel and the consistent use of allegory make its kinship to the Middle Ages strikingly apparent. Perhaps it is this aspect that induced Sean O'Casey in *Rose and Crown* to criticize the novel so devastatingly:

> Never a word, never a public word about the well known and very able catholic writer, Graham Greene's *Brighton Rock*, in which Brighton becomes a city of darkest night and darkest morn, too; in which everything and everyone seems to be on the road of evil. Talk of James Joyce! Joyce had humour, Greene has none; and in the darkest part of Joyce there are always bright flashes of light; here the very light itself is rotten. Even the blessed sun "slid off the sea like cuttlefish shot into the sky with the stain of agonies and endurance". Here the roman catholic girl of sixteen and the boy of seventeen, respectively, are the most stupid and evil mortals a man's mind could imagine.[1]

O'Casey's criticism cannot be put down to his anti-Catholic bias alone, for there is a great deal of truth in what he says. Yet it would seem that to understand *Brighton Rock*, it must be read much as a medieval allegory would be. The grotesque images of evil are as terrifying as the medieval representations of the devils, though, specifically, they owe a good deal to Eliot's *The Waste Land:* the broken windows, the ouija board, the gramophone, the Cosmopolitan Hotel, death by water—all have their counterparts in Eliot's poem.

In *Brighton Rock* Greene for the first time relates the theme of corrupted innocence, the theme of betrayal, the motif of the chase, and his own symbols of evil to a specifically religious theme: the Roman Catholicism of the central characters. Good and evil are defined in terms of the religion of the boy Pinkie and the girl Rose. The subject matter is presented in the same melodramatic convention as before: the confrontations and the coincidences still form a portion of the structure, but the chase, and the betrayal, and the confession are now determined by a religious motif.

The plot concerns the racetrack gangs and the razor slashings that accompany the protection rackets. It deals with the bookmakers, the bettors, the gamblers, and the squealers; it makes use of the jargon of the track—"polony," "buer," "carving," "bogies"; and it moves against a background of artificial gaiety—amusement booths and shooting galleries, dance halls and pavilions, piers and pubs. It moves against the sea, the traditional symbol of changeless change, of continuity. In bare outline the novel seems just another thriller: Ida Arnold, the inquisitive person who seeks natural justice; Pinkie Brown, the pursued; Rose, the love element. *Brighton Rock* has all the equipment of the thriller, but the melodramatic contrivances are integrated to give meaning to the religious importunities of the theme. Always there is the felt presence of the Church, urging, defining, commenting, never relenting. And it is this religious frame of reference that gives the novel a coherent allegorical meaning. The central theme is one of justice, of right overcoming wrong.

Pinkie Brown is the seventeen-year-old leader of Kite's mob, the same Kite whose murder was related in *A Gun for Sale*. A publicity man for the *Daily Messenger*, Fred Hale had betrayed Kite to Colleoni (whose name is borrowed from *The Aspern Papers*), a successful racketeer who is friendly with the police. To keep the mob together, Pinkie must exhibit his right of leadership by avenging Kite's murder. Fred Hale dies of heart failure before he can be "carved," but it is murder all the same.

To escape the vengeance of Pinkie and the mob, Fred, or Kolley Kibber as he is known professionally, attaches himself to Ida Arnold, a good-hearted blonde who frequents the amusement areas. When Ida leaves him for a few minutes to go to the "Ladies," Hale falls prey to Pinkie and the mob. Back in London, Ida learns of Fred's death, and, remembering his fear and his desire to live, she discounts the idea of suicide, or death by heart failure. She goes back to Brighton to discover the right and wrong of the matter and becomes involved in the gang war between Pinkie and Colleoni. She bets Fred's horse, Black Boy, and wins enough money to allow her to trap the murderer at her leisure.

To cover up Hale's murder, Pinkie had sent Spicer, an elderly and timid mobster, to leave Kolley Kibber's identification cards at various places in Brighton so that the time of the murder might not be fixed. At Snow's Restaurant, a card is found by Rose, a young waitress who knows that Spicer is not Kolley Kibber. To keep her silent, Pinkie courts her, and she falls in love with him. Ida discovers from Rose that Fred Hale had not left Kibber's card, and she places the guilt of Fred's death on Pinkie. She becomes Fred's avenger.

As her name implies, Ida is described in terms of the mother image. Fred's pride rebels at the association he makes with her, but all the same she represents the safety and darkness of the womb: "His eyes turned to the big breasts; she was like darkness to him, shelter, knowledge, common sense; his heart ached at the sight; but, in his little inky cynical framework of bone, pride bobbed up again, taunting him 'back to the womb . . . be a mother to you . . . no more standing on your own feet.' " [2] Moreover, the idea of Ida as mother is emphasized constantly throughout the novel; at one point she introduces herself to the mob as Rose's mother.

But Ida is much more than the mother image, for in the pattern of the allegory she represents humanity. She feels that she knows the difference between right and wrong, but she is ill at ease where the issue is one of good and evil. " 'I'm a sticker where right's concerned,' " she says (17). She has no religion to speak of, and in this respect she resembles Anne Crowder. Ida is vitality and strength; she believes firmly that only what she sees around her is real. She is the humanity of most people, the crowds at Brighton "having a bit of fun." Fred is correct in attaching himself to her, for she is the antithesis of the death that awaits him at Pinkie's hands. Resenting the fact that Fred has been deprived of vital existence, her humanity rushes forth to protest the injustice.

Since Ida discounts the idea of God, preferring to believe in a natural order, it is logical for her to assume the role of avenger:

"Somebody had made Fred unhappy, and somebody was going to be made unhappy in return. An eye for an eye. If you believed in God you might leave justice to him, but you couldn't trust the One, the universal spirit. Vengeance was Ida's, just as much as reward was Ida's, the soft gluey mouth affixed in taxis, the warm handclasp in cinemas, the only reward there was. *And vengeance and reward—they were both fun*" [italics mine] (44-45). She consults her ouija board and is given the sanction she needs to set about her mission. The board spells out "FRESUI-CILLEYE": " 'Why, it's as clear as clear,' " she says, " 'Fre is short for Fred and Suici for Suicide and Eye, that's what I always say —an eye for an eye and a tooth for a tooth.' " And when she says, " 'It's going to be exciting, it's going to be a bit of life. . . .' " She gives the highest praise she can (55). Since Ida believes in the natural world, within the pattern of the allegory her idea of justice is easy to understand. The idea of God's justice, however, is not so facile; right and wrong are aspects of good and evil.

Pinkie Brown believes in right too; but he believes in might controlling right. For he is a Fascist. To coition Pinkie ascribes all the ills of the world. Here the reader is reminded of Minty of *England Made Me*. As a child he had rejected his parents after witnessing their Saturday night ritual of sex. In Kite he had found a "father," for Kite had offered him a refuge from sex. The father had died, but Pinkie had prolonged his existence—"not touching liquor, biting his nails in the Kite way . . ." (293). Representing life and creation, Ida forces Pinkie to marry the waitress who had seen Spicer leave Kolley Kibber's card in Snow's Restaurant. The natural mother, within the allegory, battles the unnatural father—Ida versus Kite, love and violence opposed. For Kite represents the cult of power as Ida represents the religion of humanity. The strong man in terms of the allegory runs up against the forces of society and is defeated.

The idea of sex is tied in for Pinkie with the idea of purity, purity conditioned by his Roman Catholicism. His virginity affords a strength and the pride he would not otherwise have. Like Andrews of *The Man Within* and like Conrad Drover of *It's a Battlefield*, Pinkie is limited in his knowledge of life; but, unlike them, he has been schooled in evil by his Roman Catholicism. Pinkie believes in hell and the devil because he knows the exquisite torture of pain; suffering is for him the only reality.

[83]

When Rose asks him if he believes in hell, he answers: " 'Of course it's true . . . what else could there be? . . . Why . . . it's the only thing that fits. These Atheists, they don't know nothing. Of course, there's Hell. Flames and damnation . . . torments' " (66).

The images of damnation have been constantly with Pinkie and the sex act has become for him the index of the world's evil. Sex had caused Annie Collins to put her head on the railroad lines: " 'She had to wait ten minutes for the seven-five. Fog made it late from Victoria. Cut off her head. She was fifteen. She was going to have a baby and she knew what it was like. She'd had one two years before, and they could 'ave pinned it on twelve boys' " (219). Pinkie knows hell intimately for he sees it in life. When his lawyer Prewitt quotes from Marlowe, " 'Why this is hell, nor are we out of it,' " Pinkie looks at him with horrified interest, for he thinks that he alone knows the secret (281-82). The symbols of hell have been constantly around him: the man who collects debris along the Brighton walks, the beggar who has lost the whole of one side of the body, Rose's parents who sell her for fifteen guineas. Life for Pinkie is his parents on Saturday night. Nature that spoke to Wordsworth of "the types and symbols of eternity" speaks to Pinkie of eternity too, but of an eternity of pain, "Worms and cataract, cancer . . . children being born . . . dying slowly" (304).

Intimate with evil as he is, Pinkie can recognize its opposite when he sees it. " 'I'll be seeing you,' " he says to Rose, " 'You an' me have things in common' " (33). Rose and Pinkie are opposite sides of the same coin; one cannot exist without the other. Yet Pinkie makes the mistake of thinking that goodness and ignorance are one. He fails to perceive that Rose recognizes his evil and nevertheless loves him.

Rose and Pinkie have in common their Roman Catholicism. Coming from Nelson Place, Rose is intimate with the same symbols of evil as Pinkie; but her innocence has not been soured. What is good in her responds to what is evil in Pinkie, and she knows that he can orient himself only in respect to her: "What was most evil in him needed her: it couldn't get along without goodness" (176). Forced to corrupt goodness when he marries Rose to keep her from testifying, Pinkie betrays his virginity, the source of his strength, as he betrays his putative father. Theirs is the marriage of heaven and hell: "She was good, he'd discovered that, and he was damned: they were made for each other" (168).

In terms of the allegory, the chief polarities of good and evil are established by Rose and Pinkie; the middle ground is represented by Ida Arnold. And Ida is able to recognize how alien these two extremes are to her world of man. When with Pinkie and Rose, she feels as though she is in a strange country; and she hasn't even a phrase book to help her understand their language. As the representative of human nature, she can distinguish between right and wrong—or so she thinks; but she feels her inadequacy when the issue is one of extreme good or extreme evil. She is indeed an alien in the spiritual drama she precipitates, for the mercy and justice of God are beyond her comprehension. For her everything is life and vitality; justice to be determined in the world is an eye for an eye, a tooth for a tooth.

Ida has as her allies the forces of continuity, Pinkie the forces of the devil to whom he is dedicated. Time and again he says, "*Credo in unum Satanum.*" His energy is as potent as Ida's, but he has chosen to channel it for evil rather than for good. In his limited knowledge of life, in his search for peace—the refrain he constantly sings is "*Dona eis pacem*"—peace and power are synonymous; yet his Catholicism has taught him that each step on the way to power places another nail in the body of Christ. He had thought to channel this energy for good when, as a child, he had wished to be a priest. Celibacy would have been a safeguard against coition, but Kite and the evil he saw dominant in the world about him had won him away from holiness. Ida forces Pinkie to commit himself to the natural world, the world of sex.

If justice in the world is to be asserted, Pinkie and his evil must be destroyed. And Ida, humanity, must bring this destruction about. The forces of vitality ally themselves with her when Black Boy wins the race, as Fred Hale had said he would. Pinkie recognizes the moment: "'If I was one of those crazy geezers who touch wood, throw salt, go under ladders, I might be scared to——'" (138). From the moment of the race his plans are made with extreme care, but his every step is conditioned by a pressure he can't even place. Ida asks questions, she calls Spicer on the phone, she badgers Rose. Pinkie seeks to stem the tide by marrying Rose, by corrupting her to his own evil, by asking her to submit to a sham suicide pact. But this is not enough, for Ida is relentless: "'Look at me,'" she says, "'I've never changed. It's like those sticks of rock: bite it all the way down, you'll still read Brighton. That's human nature'" (266). She rushes to the cliff where Pinkie is forcing damnation on Rose; the policeman with her is bewildered, yet he must do as she commands. She forestalls Rose's suicide and forces Pinkie to his death—and his damnation.

When the drama is ended, Rose goes to her confessor and insists that she is unable to repent her failure to damn herself alongside Pinkie. The priest speaks to her of Péguy, the "sinner" who could not accept the thought that God would allow any of his creatures to suffer damnation; he speaks to her of the "appalling strangeness of the mercy of God" (331-32). His is the voice of the Church, attempting to reestablish a mean once the passions of men have spent themselves. He intercedes to comfort the living, and he asks Rose to "hope and pray," for the Church does not demand that anyone believe that a soul may be cut off from mercy. He makes the final commentary on the action when he says, "'. . . a Catholic is more capable of evil than anyone. I think perhaps—because we believe in Him—we are more in touch with the devil than other people'" (332). But Rose is uncertain, for her knowledge of evil has taught her the reality of damnation. Certain that she carries Pinkie's child within her, she goes home "to the worst horror of all"—the record Pinkie had made for her on which he had told her how much he hated her and what she represented (333). This is the worst horror of all, that Rose must return to life: life without hope, world without end. Once the drama is ended, evil seems the order of the universe, as continuous as life itself. Pinkie falls into the sea; the sea absorbs his evil, and it becomes a portion of the natural world. Life for Rose becomes a "horror," for, with the knowledge of Pinkie's hatred, she is denied hope.

The use of the sensational and the melodramatic in *Brighton Rock* permits Greene to present his theme in terms compatible with his religious thesis. The frame of the detective story sustains the allegorical level of meaning. Since his polarities are so sharply defined, the form of the novel emphasizes the distinctions and underscores their cogency. He uses background as symbol and for effect, and the storm in which Pinkie dies emphasizes the turmoil of the drama. Yet the storm does not cleanse, except that it exerts its peculiar influence on the reader. Following upon _A Gun for Sale_, it demonstrates to what extent the religious note can animate Greene's narrative.

II The Power and the Glory

In an essay entitled "The Young Dickens," Graham Greene says of the world of Dickens, with specific reference to _Oliver Twist:_

This world of Dickens is a world without God; and as a substitute for the power and the glory of the omnipotent and the omniscient are a few sentimental references to heaven, angels, and the sweet faces of the dead. . . . In this Manichaean world we can believe in evil doing, but goodness wilts into philanthropy, kindness, and those strange vague sicknesses into which Dickens's young women so frequently fall and which seems in his eyes a kind of badge of virtue, as though there were a merit in death.[3]

In _The Power and the Glory_ (1940), Greene employs an ingenious but sometimes heavy-handed satire that allows him to portray in the uncommon and startling guise of melodramatic allegory the power and the glory of God through his two central characters. The whiskey priest, representative of the old, corrupt, and God-ridden world of religion, and the lieutenant of the new political order, representative of the enlightened and philanthropic world of a power cult, are doubles in the Dostoevskian and Conradian sense. The differences that exist in these two symbolic figures are satirically antithetical, each suggesting what the other should be, each accenting the pity that is in the other while denying the evil. The immediate implications of the differences in the portrayals of the whiskey priest and the lieutenant are satiric; but ultimately, by suggesting the dedication of each man to a common cause, they are ironic, for Greene wishes to render the highest justice to both points of view.

The Power and the Glory, a Mexican adventure story developed on the theme of flight and pursuit, grew out of Greene's firsthand experience of Mexican politics and religion. In _The Lawless Roads_, published in 1939, Greene describes his journey of the previous year through Tabasco and Chiapas, provinces in which the Church was persecuted. Many of the characters and settings that comprise the allegory that is the novel are drawn from life, and their counterparts are to be found in the travel narrative. Dr. Tench, the dentist, grew out of Greene's acquaintance with many dentists, for toothache seems a common ailment in Mexico. The troublesome stomach Greene observed in another dentist, "small bitter exiled widower, caged in his Victorian *sala,* with the vultures routing on his roof."[4] Mr. and Miss Lehr, the German brother and sister who befriend the whiskey priest, have their counterparts in Herr R. and his sister; and, like the Lehrs of the novel, they pacified the terrorists by giving them five hundred acres of worthless land, keeping the productive soil for themselves. Their refuge is the same that Greene had actually come upon, cross and ill from his wanderings on muleback. The stream where the modest Miss Lehr bathes, the earthenware pitcher on the veranda, all are details drawn from the novelist's experience. The precocious child, Coral Fellows, derives from Fru R.'s daughter, the little girl who learned her lessons at her mother's side from a mail-order textbook. And the chief character of the novel, the whiskey priest, is developed from a casual remark made to Greene by his dentist friend, Dr. Fitzpatrick: " 'Oh,' he said, 'he was just what we call a whiskey priest.' He had taken one of his sons to be baptized, but the priest was drunk and would insist on naming him Brigitta. He was little loss, poor man . . . but who can judge what terror and hardship and isolation may have excused him in the eyes of God?" (161).

The tapestry-like quality of the landscape, the huts and the dust, the mules and the flies, the gaseosa stalls, the vultures, the sharks, the carrion—all are contained within the pages of the travel narrative: "It was like the grave, the earth taking over before its time" (208). The atmosphere of death and decay pervades the novel, and the image of the carious mouth is constantly juxtaposed with the image of the Eucharist—taking God in the mouth; and both contribute to the allegorical significance of the novel.

What interests Greene in both *The Lawless Roads* and the allegorical novel is the attitude of the Mexican state to religion. At the time Greene visited Chiapas and Tabasco, the government was Socialist in intention, but Fascist in method. He quotes in *The Lawless Roads* from Article 3 of the Constitution: " 'The education imparted by the State shall be a Socialistic one, and in addition to excluding all religious doctrine, shall combat fanaticism and prejudices by organizing its instructions and activities in a way that shall permit the creation in youth of an exact and rational conception of the Universe and social life' " (90). Forced to comply with the tenets of this new order which, indeed, can be defined as a cult of power, many of the priests married, as does Father José in the novel; and many gladly accepted martyrdom. A few preferred to minister to the people while avoiding arrest at the hands of the police. In outlawing the influence of the Church and in making any practice of its dogma an act of treason, the government sought to establish a state that would consider the bodily needs of the people and free them from the narrow-mindedness and bigotry of the Church. It sought to force the people to accept a secular in place of a religious order. But the attempt failed, for the new order could not destroy the forms and symbols of the old. Even the art that sought to exalt the state and edify the populace denied the possibility. In *The Lawless Roads* Greene describes a Rivera mural:

Rivera contributes only one moral with typical grandiloquence—all outstretched arms and noble faces, white robes and haloes. It is called "Creation": it is full of literary symbols—the Tree of Life, Dionysius, Man, Woman, Music, Comedy, Dance, Tragedy, Science, Temperance, Fortitude. It adapts Christian emblems to a vague political idea, and they become unbearably sentimental in the new setting, far more sentimental than repository art. The pale blue Madonna with the seven swords does, however inadequately, represent an exact idea: but the Son in Rivera's "Creation"—what is he but Progress, Human Dignity, great empty Victorian conceptions that life denies at every turn? This is Rivera's way—to try to get the best out of both worlds. He is the Leighton or Watts of the Revolution. (86-87)

In *The Power and the Glory* Greene asserts the vitality of the Roman Catholic Church, and he attempts to explain the value of its beliefs. For all his weaknesses the whiskey priest becomes the representative not only of his Church but of the cumulative wisdom of the past; in short, of Western humanism. This does not mean, however, that *The Power and the Glory* is either a thesis novel, a saint's life, or a political tract. Rather it is a consistent allegory on the theme of Everyman. And the priest while determining the means of his salvation becomes a man fighting the unifying but degrading urges of a power cult.

The physical structure of the novel is a simple one. The first section deals with the bystanders, those whom the priest touches in his flight. They are Dr. Tench, the dentist; Coral Fellows, the precocious child; Luis, whose mother offers shelter to the fugitive; the Chief of Police; and the lieutenant, the representative of the power cult. Neither the lieutenant nor the priest is named, so as not to intrude on the allegorical importunities of the major theme. The second section deals with the priest's flight from the civil authorities, and it introduces the *mestizo*, the Judas of the allegory. The third section begins with a peaceful interlude, a limbo amidst the melodramatic activities of the novel, during which the priest is in danger of falling back into the complacent ways of his early ministry; and it develops his decision to accept his martyrdom. At this point the theme of flight and pursuit is reversed so that the priest may become the aggressor and the champion of his convictions. Through the priest Greene develops his major theme: the grace of God exerted on the soul of a man whose weakness is, paradoxically, the symbol of his strength. And the figure of the priest allows Greene to work within the anatomy of sainthood.

In *Brighton Rock* Greene defined his religious preoccupations in terms of allegory: he personified good and evil in Rose and Pinkie. Rose was the central character in this symbolic drama, but, more often than not, her goodness was overshadowed by Pinkie's more fascinating evil. Having defined his poles in *Brighton Rock*, Greene could go on to combine good and evil in a single individual as he does in *The Power and the Glory*. His remark on Frederick Rolfe, Baron Corvo, bears quoting here: "The greatest saints have been men with more than a normal capacity for evil, and the most vicious men have sometimes narrowly escaped sancitity." [5]

In *The Power and the Glory* Greene chose a striking method of presenting his theme. On the allegorical level the novel is the whiskey priest's attempt to avoid sainthood. The alternative title to the novel, *The Labyrinthine Ways*—an allusion to Thompson's "The Hound of Heaven"—indicates that the priest's flight is a flight from God and that the journey he makes is one of self-recognition. Greene makes brilliant use of counterpoint as he describes the priest's flight from the authorities, which is at the same time his evasion of grace. Only after he is betrayed by the half-caste Judas can the whiskey priest fully accept his destiny. It is at that moment that the theme of flight and pursuit is reversed, and the lieutenant becomes the pursued. This figure eight pattern is one of Greene's favorites.

Within the framework of the allegory the poles represented by the whiskey priest and the lieutenant are arranged in a satiric fashion; the secular order is represented by the lieutenant, the religious by the priest. The lieutenant's power is, understandably, the source of his belief; and he accepts the violence and brutality that this power engenders as necessary and rational concomitants of his faith. He is temperate, completely certain of the value of his creed. He is strong, resolute, and dedicated. He has self-respect. And he is celibate. As he exercises his power, he puts killing down to love. In short, he is everything that the whiskey priest should be and is not.

At the opposite polarity the priest is a drunkard who periodically seeks to evade his responsibility. There is the smell of decay about him, and the vulture hovers over him as a token of his destiny. When the reader first sees him, he is attempting to flee Mexico; and Dr. Tench, a bystander, is reminded of death: "The man's dark suit and sloping shoulders reminded him uncomfortably of a coffin, and death was in his carious mouth already." [6] He is a coward, and a creature of habit; his great sin is his illegitimate daughter Brigitta, the offspring of his loneliness and pride. Yet the differences between these two men are ultimately points of irony rather than of satire. For Greene, in holding up to contempt the deficiencies of one man, nevertheless caricatures the virtues of the other. Neither is a hero in the traditional sense, yet both portray the force of their convictions.

The destiny of the whiskey priest is implied from the novel's beginning when in the police station the lieutenant places the priest's photograph next to that of the American gangster who assumes the role of Nemesis. The lieutenant says approvingly of the gangster, " 'He is a man at any rate' " (23). The lieutenant looks at the priest's photograph, taken ten years before at a Communion party; and he feels his responsibility keenly as he dedicates himself to his task of ridding his country of the pernicious influence of the priest's Church: "He had the dignity of an idea, standing in the little whitewashed room with his polished boots and his venom. There was something disinterested in his ambition: a kind of virtue in his desire to catch the sleek respected guest of the first communion party" (23).

The lieutenant is described as "a theologian going back over the errors of the past to destroy them again" (25). He is indeed the priest of the political order that promises as its sacraments food, clothing, and security instead of misery, poverty, and superstition. And it infuriates him to think that there are people who believe in the myth of a merciful God. The lieutenant's life had begun for him on a day five years before the action of the novel when he had been ordained to destroy the canker of religion. And yet, for all his weaknesses, it is the priest who carries the seeds of redemption.

The priest comes to an appreciation of God in Man during the night he spends in a crowded prison cell, a microcosm of his world. In the filth and stench he sees human nature at its lowest; and he identifies the evil in the world with that in himself. As one woman harangues the priest to hear her confession and as two prisoners find comfort in the sexual act, their cries of pleasure reminding him of his weakness and of his daughter Brigitta, the priest sees the people of God, and he understands more clearly than ever before the condition of His kingdom. In the lovers and the other inmates he sees the types and symbols of eternity: " 'Such a lot of beauty. Saints talk a lot about the beauty of suffering. Well, we are not saints, you and I. Suffering is to us just ugly. Stench and crowding and pain. *That* is beautiful in the corner—to them. It needs a lot of learning to see things with a saint's eye; a saint gets a subtle taste for beauty and can look down on poor ignorant palates like theirs. But we can't afford to' " (168). Wedged in beside an old man who murmurs about an illegitimate daughter, the priest is overcome by an overwhelming pity for suffering and misery. He remembers from experience the beauty of evil: " 'how much beauty Satan carried down with him when he fell' " (169). He sees and feels God in the poor and the helpless; and he finds it possible to pity the half-caste who seeks to betray him.

Having found his own kind, the whiskey priest feels the need of confession. As he tells his fellow prisoners that he is a whiskey priest and the father of a child, he longs for the simplicity of death. He prays for Brigitta, although he knows in his heart that the evil in her is too fixed to be overcome. Yet in his dedication to her, he begins to orient himself into the scheme of God; he opens his heart to grace, and he begins his journey of recognition.

The next morning, while still in prison, the priest comes face to face with his antagonist, the lieutenant, for the second time—the first encounter had taken place in the priest's village. But the lieutenant does not recognize him either as a priest or as the man he had met in the village, the father of the child Brigitta. Touched by the old man who has no money, the lieutenant gives the priest five pesos, ironically the price of a mass. Astonished, the priest says, " 'You're a good man' " (181).

When he leaves the prison, the priest goes to the home of Coral Fellows, the child who had befriended him earlier and who is, symbolically, his "good" daughter, to discover that she has died. He goes on until he comes upon an Indian mother whose child has been shot three times by that same American gangster, James Calver (the name suggests Calvary, of course), whose photograph had been placed beside his in the police station. The rains come, and the priest is spiritually cleansed. He recognizes the primitive simplicity and the quiet beauty of the Indian mother's belief as she places a lump of hard, brown sugar beside the body of her slaughtered child. Since his release from prison, the priest had fallen in a state of limbo; and his aimless wanderings indicate the searchings of his soul. Since his experiences in the prison had opened his heart to grace, the rain symbolizes his soul's state. Delirious, he is found by a peasant who takes him across the border into a province where there is religious tolerance.

Mr. and Miss Lehr nurse him to health; and the priest decides that, since he has crossed the border and is no longer subject to the jurisdiction of the lieutenant, he will give up his life of wandering ministrant, go to Las Casas, and secure the formal forgiveness of his Church in confession. But he begins to fall back into the arrogant and slothful ways of his youth, and he forgets what he has learned from suffering. Appalled, he welcomes the *mestizo* and the betrayal that awaits him; for after such knowledge as his, the priest knows there can be no forgiveness. The half-caste tells the fugitive that the American gangster has been shot by the police and is asking for a priest. The wounded man had written a note on the back of one of Coral's school exercises—an exercise concerning Hamlet's inability to act once he knows Claudius to be his father's murderer, an interesting coun- terpoint to the main action of the melodrama. The priest hums the song about a rose in a field that he had first heard while attempt- ing to escape on the *General Obregon* at the novel's beginning.[7] As the priest welcomes his Judas, he becomes the pursuer; and his antagonist, the lieutenant, the pursued.

Over the body of the American gangster, the advocate of the religious order, for the first time in full command of his ministry, opposes the priest of the secular order. This is their third en- counter. The satiric poles are charged over the body of Nemesis, and a dramatic debate ensues. The lieutenant argues that the priest, although himself a good man, is a danger to the well-being of the state and that his destruction is necessary to secure that well-being. He insists that the priest's religion does not free peo- ple from want and misery, and that his does. " 'We'll give them food instead,' " he says, " 'teach them to read, give them books. We'll see that they don't suffer' " (251). To this the priest makes the only answer he can. The poor, he says, are in greatest favor with God, and the kingdom of heaven is theirs. He agrees with the lieutenant that the only certainty of life is death, but he dis- agrees with him as to what constitutes the essence of living. He points out that he who rules through power and fear is open to the temptations of power and fear; and he insists that unless the minister of the secular order maintain his motives in honesty and truth, nothing but corruption can result from his office: " 'It's no good your working for your end unless you are a good man your- self. And there won't always be good men in your party. But it doesn't matter so much my being a coward—and all the rest. I can put God in a man's mouth just the same—and I can give him God's pardon. It wouldn't make any difference to that if ev- ery priest in the Church was like me' " (252-53).

The difference in their beliefs comes down to the simple fact that the priest has perfection as his point of reference. " 'It's bet- ter to let the poor die in dirt and wake in heaven,' " he says (258). And here Greene's satire on the political order is made explicit. Once the lieutenant has clothed and fed the body and pushed the face of the poor into the dirt to do so—forced them to accept the "sacraments" of political "progress"—what is left but another religion, one that replaces humility and decency and love with fear and violence and despair? The priest insists that unless authority begins from perfection, from God, it will breed corruption. And he goes on to point out that there will not always be good men in the lieutenant's party. Speaking with the authority of his Church, the priest is nevertheless aware of his inadequacies as a man; and he has found the mercy of God incomprehensible: " 'I don't know a thing about the mercy of God: I don't know how awful the human heart looks to him. But I do know this—that if there's ever been a single man in this state damned, then I'll be damned too. . . . I wouldn't want it to be any different. I just want justice, that's all' " (259).

The motif is again from Péguy; Greene had used it in the epilogue scene of *Brighton Rock* when the priest had asked Rose to hope and pray. Rose's suffering had told her that Pinkie was damned, and the lieutenant's intelligence tells him that if there is salvation, the priest is saved. Impressed with the sincerity of the priest, the lieutenant promises to ask Father José, the conformist, to hear the whiskey priest's confession, even if it means a "triumph for that old corrupt God-ridden world."

It is their pity for suffering that both the whiskey priest and the man of power have in common; and they realize too that they will never be able to agree. This again is an aspect of the novel's satire, heavy-handed though it may seem. The lieutenant in giving in to the priest's plea for a confessor feels his weakness, but he refuses to acknowledge it as an index of his strength. The priest has lived in the shadow of plenitude, but the lieutenant has experienced vacancy. When Father José refuses to hear the fugitive's confession, the secular order seems to triumph; but strangely, the lieutenant experiences the sensation of vacancy as he never has before. The priest has touched the heart of the man; but in the pursuit of his duty the lieutenant is inflexible. And indeed he must remain so or tear the fabric of the allegory; his capitulation would mean the submission of the power cult to God.

In having submitted to the will of God, the priest had come to an understanding of God in the phenomenal world. Alone in his cell while awaiting execution, he discovers that his love for human beings extends only to Brigitta, his evil daughter. And he attempts to bargain with God, offering his damnation for her salvation. He resents the fact that the child who had nothing to do with desiring life is to be damned. He himself is the cause of her evil—he can hate his sin, but he cannot hate the result of 't.

As he thinks of his inability to love all living things, he feels that he has failed God again and that he will approach Him empty-handed. He dreams of Coral Fellows, his "good" daughter, and he sees her as his advocate at the throne of God. In the last moments he realizes the enormity of human failings, and his tears are those of genuine contrition.

But the priest does not go to God empty-handed. Unknown to him he has touched the hearts of three, perhaps four, bystanders: the child Coral; the boy Luis; Mr. Tench, the dentist; and he has made the lieutenant aware of his emptiness. Coral had seen the crosses that the fugitive had left on the wall of the banana barn, and with her first menstrual pain the realization of God in the world had come to her—pain, suffering. Bored by the romanticized saints' lives his mother has been reading him, the boy Luis begins to understand true heroism through the execution of the priest. As the lieutenant walks by, feeling his emptiness, he sees the boy and remembers that just such a one had toyed with his pistol a few weeks before. Luis spits at him, and the spittle lands on the holster. That night the boy admits another fugitive priest to his mother's house. Dr. Tench watches the execution from the Chief of Police's window—he has come to remove an infected tooth. As he sees the fugitive die, he determines to leave the country, to return to England, and to set his lands in order. The priest leaves the impression of his heroism on three hearts, and he also shows the lieutenant the possibility of salvation.

Perhaps the chief criticism that has been aimed at *The Power and the Glory* is that it is narrowly Roman Catholic. I do not think this is so. The whiskey priest is a Roman Catholic, but what he represents transcends the narrow limits of any one religious belief. The fact that he is a Catholic intensifies the conflict of the novel and lends dignity to its action. As the fugitive battles the lieutenant and the organized violence that he symbolizes, the Church fades into the background. The priest becomes an individual fighting a guerrilla war for what he believes to be right. And while finding out, like Everyman, the ways and means of his salvation, he succeeds in setting up a reaction as continuous as life itself. In the character of the priest, Greene again approaches the quality of myth.

III   The Heart of the Matter

Everyone who has read Graham Greene's *The Heart of the Matter* has become aware in one way or another of the critical furor occasioned by the religious issues arising from the suicide of the hero, Major Scobie. Evelyn Waugh wrote in *The Commonweal* upon publication of *The Heart of the Matter:* "To me the idea of willing my own damnation for the love of God is either a very loose poetical expression or a mad blasphemy, for the God who accepted that sacrifice could be neither just nor lovable." [8] But it is not the purpose here to paraphrase those critics who for various reasons have accused Greene of being everything from a Manichaean to an Existentialist. Many readers of *The Heart of the Matter* have made the serious error of attempting to abstract from its pages Greene's personal philosophy or religious belief. Insisting on a prerogative of philosophical and theological speculation, critics and "fans" alike have failed to recognize that in his serious novels Greene creates an experience of life which is not representative of a religious bias but of a *"condition humaine."* Considering his position as a Catholic writer, Greene's statement to Elizabeth Bowen bears repetition. Greene says, the reader will remember, that literature has nothing to do with edification. He argues that literature is not amoral but that it represents a personal moral, and that the personal morality of an individual is seldom identical with the morality of the group to which he belongs.

As novelist, Greene feels that he must be free to write as he wishes, that he must give doubt, and even denial, self-expression. If he cannot do so, he is no freer than a Communist propagandist.[9]

The point to consider in a discussion of *The Heart of the Matter* is not why Greene uses a religious theme but how; it is important to decide whether or not his use of a religious theme invalidates the novel as a work of art. And to do so, Greene must be considered as a novelist who is a Catholic, not as a dilettante of religion and theology, or, to repeat his statement in his essay on the religious aspect of Henry James, "a philosopher or religious teacher of the second rank." The problem then of whether Major Scobie is "saved" or not according to the teachings of the Catholic Church becomes a minor consideration; for the novel presents a personal moral—Scobie's moral—which may not coincide with that of orthodox Catholicism.

Scobie's struggle within himself and with the God of the Catholic Church forms the basis of the conflict: Scobie's pity for suffering humanity forces him to suicide, the sin of despair. And according to the Church, this is damnation. As Greene's ablest critics, Kenneth Allott and Miriam Farris, point out, "Discussion of the meaning of *The Heart of the Matter* is doomed in advance to sterility if it does not take into account that the words composing the book have been organized primarily with an artistic, rather than a philosophical or theological, intention." [10] But it is equally wrong for Allott and Farris to minimize the importance of the religious theme, for it is the frame of reference within which the narrative develops. Neglecting the spiritual conflict within Scobie reduces the novel to a structural *tour de force;* these critics do not appreciate fully the intense spiritual drama which is the novel's reason for being. They diminish the aspect of recognition and misunderstand the theme of betrayal, interwoven with Scobie's intense love of God, which are fundamental to the comprehension of the book.[11] It is more nearly correct to accept Scobie's Catholicism as something akin to the Fatality of Greek drama.

For Major Scobie, as for Arthur Rowe, the hero of *The Ministry of Fear,* pity is the keynote of human existence: "What an absurd thing it was to expect happiness in a world so full of misery. . . . If one knew, he wondered, the facts, would one have to feel pity even for the planets? if one reached what they called the heart of the matter?" [12] The imagery of the novel corresponds to the intensity of the pity and formulates the mood. References to rusty handcuffs, broken rosaries (side by side in Scobie's desk), swollen pye-dogs, joints of meat, cannon fodder—all eventually resolve themselves into an overwhelming sense of decay. The broken rosary and the rusty handcuffs become symbolic of divine justice opposing human justice. Scobie stands in relationship to his sphere as God does to His. The vulture hovers over Scobie, implying not the terror of death—as it does for the whiskey priest in *The Power and the Glory*—but the terror of life and the remoteness of death: "Couldn't the test of man have been carried out in fewer years? Couldn't we have committed our first major sin at seven, have ruined ourselves for love or hate at ten, have clutched at redemption on a fifteen-year-old death-bed?" (56).

The Major Novels

The setting of the novel, West Africa, allows for this kind of imaginative painting. The rain and the steam, the atabrine-yellow faces, the gangrenous flesh, all indicate a languor and ennui which allow for an explosion of any kind. There is an implicit tension, for the reader is ever conscious of World War II through the hostility that exists between the English sector and the Vichy French sector across the river. The sense of history and the threat of violence are neatly compressed, as in classical drama, into the relationships that exist among a few people. The individual struggle is of first importance; the imagery and the setting form a portion of that Necessity which propels Scobie on his quest of recognition. The dramatic construction of the plot, moreover, accommodates the inevitability of the catastrophe.

A middle-aged police officer in British West Africa, Major Scobie, a member of Greene's "awkward squad," one who has had no opportunity to break the more serious military rules, is passed over for promotion (9). His wife Louise, for whom he feels only pity and responsibility, urges him to allow her to go for a holiday to South Africa, to escape the malice of her "friends." To avoid making her unhappy, Scobie borrows from Yusef, a merchant suspected of diamond smuggling by Wilson, the British agent who fancies himself in love with Louise. It is suggested that Yusef is the evil aspect of Scobie, and indeed he becomes the tool of Necessity.

A torpedoed ship brings Helen Rolt into the pattern of Scobie's unhappiness. He sees her carried on shore, after forty days in an open boat, clutching her stamp album like a child. And he falls in love with her because she is pathetic: "Against the beautiful and the clever and the successful, one can wage a pitiless war, but not against the unattractive: then the millstone weighs on the breast" (53). The situation builds up into the eternal triangle; and it is a credit to Greene's artistry that he is able to pour heady wine into such an old barrel. Scobie soon realizes that his love for Helen is only another facet of his pity. He realizes that Helen is Louise and Louise is Helen, and that he is equally responsible for the happiness of both: "Pity smoldered like decay at his heart. . . . He knew from experience how passion died away and how love went, but pity always stayed. Nothing ever diminished pity. The conditions of life nurtured it" (211). After an argument he writes Helen a note: "I love you more than myself, more than my wife, more than God I think" (215). The note falls into the hands of Yusef, who blackmails Scobie into smuggling diamonds for him.

When Louise returns from South Africa, Wilson blurts out that Scobie and Helen are lovers. To see whether or not Scobie has given up his mistress, Louise insists that he accompany her to Communion. How simple it would be, he thinks, if he could withdraw his pity from Helen, repent his sin in the confessional, and free himself of responsibility. But he is too honest to pretend a repentance he does not feel. His confessor, Father Rank, is merely an intermediary; Scobie knows that the brief rests with God, and he will not add hypocrisy to his other sins. He knows that he must crucify either God or Louise. The suffering of God, however, is unreal, remote; that of Louise is nearer—he can feel her pain and also Helen's. He chooses sacrilege and damnation by taking Communion without having received absolution at confession: " 'O God I offer my damnation to you. Take it. Use it for them' " (272).

With the sacrilege comes the commissionership that Louise has so long coveted. Now "of the devil's party," Scobie knows that he will go from "damned success to damned success" (276); and he indulges in the bitter jest. With the smuggling of the diamonds comes his realization that he is "one of those whom people pity" and his further awareness that his corruption corrupts others (244). He tacitly agrees to the murder of his boy Ali by one of Yusef's killers. He knows that he has destroyed to keep from bringing hurt to either Helen or Louise, and he determines to set them free of him. He reasons that, if he kills himself, he will stop crucifying God; and it is God whom he loves above all things:

. . . O God, I am the only guilty one because I've known the answers all the time. I've preferred to give you pain rather than give pain to Helen or my wife because I can't observe your suffering. I can only imagine it. But there are limits to· what I can do to—or them. I can't desert either of them while I am alive, but I can die and remove myself from their blood stream. They are ill with me. . . . I can't go on, month after month, insulting you. I can't face coming up to the altar at Christmas—your birthday feast—and taking your body and blood for the sake of a lie. I can't do that. You'll be better off if you lose me once and for all.   (315)

He will hurt God once and for all—deprive God of himself as he will deprive himself of God. A voice within tempts him to virtue as to sin: "You say you love me, and yet you'll do this to me—rob me of you forever. I made you with love. . . . And now you push me away, you put me out of your reach." Scobie answers, "No. I don't trust you. I love you, but I've never trusted you. If you made me, you made this feeling of responsibility that I've carried about like a sack of bricks" (316-17). This is Scobie's sin: he prefers to trust himself, in his limited knowledge of love, rather than God, who is all love. He cannot put his faith in trust of God; for his faith is love and pity is its image. Scobie cannot comprehend the "appalling" nature of the mercy of God. He knows that the choice for damnation is his alone as he drinks the narcotic. He hears someone calling for him, a cry of distress; automatically he stirs himself to act. Aloud he says, " 'Dear God, I love . . .' " (326).

At the end of the novel Father Rank returns to give comfort to the living, to reestablish the norm of the Church and to give hope for Scobie's soul, even though he committed suicide. " 'The Church knows all the rules,' " he says. " 'But it doesn't know what goes on in a single human heart' " (333). He insists that, if Louise has forgiven Scobie, then God can be no less forgiving. Louise remarks that Scobie really loved no one but God, and the reader remembers how often Scobie had been struck by the truth of her perceptions.

The Heart of the Matter takes its epigraph from Péguy: "Le pécheur est au cœur même de chrétienté . . . Nul n'est aussi compétent que le pécheur en matière de chrétienté. Nul, si ce n'est le saint." Major Scobie's pity, his love, becomes indicative of a universal love; it is in matters of trust that he fails. In the process of learning the wherewithal of his religion, he realizes the immensity of human love, but he fails to recognize the immensity of the mercy of God. His pride and his humility conspire against him, and, because he cannot trust the God he loves, he commits the sin of despair. In matters of his religion he has become competent, for according to Greene the sinner is very close to God.

In an interesting essay published in *Transformation Three,* Martin C. D'Arcy discusses the anatomy of the hero within a Christian context:

In the Christian scale of values the hero is not easily distinguishable from the saint; it is more a matter of emphasis than of division. The saint cannot be canonized unless he can be shown to have practiced heroic virtues; the man of heroic deeds cannot be called a hero unless there is evidence that his inner spirit corresponds with his deeds, and that his motives are pure. But whereas in using the word saint, the emphasis is on a man's relation to God and his spiritual work for his fellow man, it is prowess and self-sacrifice for others, for friends or a nation, which is uppermost in our thought of the hero.[13]

D'Arcy goes on to point out what C. Day Lewis in *A Hope for Poetry* and Rex Warner in *The Cult of Power* had pointed out: The social organism has grown to such a size that it has complicated man's relationship with the other life, and man has come to associate his limitations with the state. The potentiality of tragic action in either the classical or the Elizabethan sense is limited because the individual no longer finds means to battle so complex and bewildering an organism. The Aristotelian concept of tragic flaw or error in judgment no longer appertains. It is something of this problem that Franz Kafka dramatizes in his works, particularly in *The Trial* and in *The Castle*. Such "heroes" created by Arthur Miller as Willy Loman in *Death of a Salesman* and Joe Keller in *All My Sons* and, more recently, the airman in Terence Rattigan's *The Deep Blue Sea* become at best pitiful characters. However, if the frame of reference within which the character moves is defined, if the antagonist is shown to be a noble one, and if the protagonist has some idea of the force he opposes and why he opposes it, then the possibility for heroism is no longer limited. The error in judgment or the tragic flaw may once again become considerations. The hero can be as tragic as he was in Greek drama or in Elizabethan tragedy.

This is the case with Scobie. He knows his antagonist, and he recognizes his strength. What he cannot accept is the orthodox Roman Catholic conception of God. For Scobie suffering and love are irreconcilable. He cannot fathom a God who seems not to love those whom He has created, a God who has not the same sense of pity and responsibility as himself. Scobie can love infinite goodness, but he cannot trust it since it allows unreasonable anguish. And in *The Heart of the Matter* Greene's daring is incredible: he pits the individual against God. Scobie becomes at once a traitor, a scapegoat, and a hero; his sense of pity, an image of his love for God, assumes the proportions of a tragic flaw. It is incontestable that he suffers more than he deserves; but whether or not he is damned becomes unimportant in a consideration of his heroism. Yusef becomes Necessity, for he makes the tragedy inevitable; and Catholicism hangs over the novel like the Fatality of Greek drama. Pity and fear are aroused in the reader, and Greene wisely leaves the issue of damnation open at the end. What is important is that Scobie by pleading for humanity opposes God and is defeated, and his excessive pity makes him a truly tragic figure.

The reference to *Othello*, furthermore, appears in the novel for a very good reason. When Yusef, the evil that is in Scobie, says, " 'I am the base Indian,' " Scobie realizes that his integrity, the pearl worth all his tribe, has been bartered for the happiness of Helen and Louise (242). He makes the mistake of thinking that he can arrange the happiness of others, but he knows in his heart that "no one can arrange another's happiness," for experience has taught him this (93). Like Othello, Scobie loves not wisely but too well. The human entanglement in which he finds himself admits only one solution—suicide. To discuss whether or not Othello is damned is absurd, but Greene invites such discussion when he pits Scobie against God. One hopes that both Scobie and Othello are, at worst, in a special limbo reserved for literary heroes.

In the light of this conflict with God, it is necessary to accept the religious theme as primary and all other considerations as secondary. It is precisely because Scobie's heroism depends so strongly on a Roman Catholic frame of reference that Father Rank cannot be dismissed as the mere plot contrivance that Allott and Farris consider him. Father Rank must attempt to restore the norm of the Church; its doctrines must be presented as flexible enough to accommodate heroic action: the Church may know all the rules but not what goes on in a human heart. Scobie may have killed himself, but he may have repented in the moment before death. Father Rank's presence is indispensable to the plan of the novel, for Greene's dramatic technique in the construction of plot demands, as has been noted, that someone restore balance and order in the world after the passions of men have spent themselves. At the end of *Othello*, Lodovico reestablishes law on the island of Cyprus and returns to Venice to relate with sorry heart the heavy deed that loads the tragic bed.

But the analogy must not be pressed too far. The contexts

within which the two dramas occur are quite alien. Othello is a man of noble deeds because his society has fostered such nobility. Scobie is a little man who becomes capable of heroism because of a sense of pity. Like Prometheus, he chooses to defy God.

IV   The End of the Affair

The End of the Affair, following upon the entertainment *The Third Man,* demonstrates a still further stage in Greene's development. The melodramatic and allegorical contrivances of *Brighton Rock* and the dramatic technique of *The Heart of the Matter* are replaced by many of the devices of the modern novel: the emotionally involved narrator, the stream-of-consciousness technique, the flashback, the diary, the letter, the inner reverie, and the spiritual debate.

The End of the Affair is the most Jamesian of Greene's novels and also the one which most suggests the influence of Mauriac on his work.[14]

In his review of Mauriac's *La Pharisienne,* Greene had written, "[With] the death of James the religious sense was lost to the English novel, and with the religious sense went the sense of the importance of the human act." To this he added that novelists after James and Flaubert had taken refuge in the subjective novel and that the characters of E. M. Forster and Virginia Woolf "wandered like cardboard symbols through a world that was paper-thin." [15] Greene went on to imply that the novel since the 1930's has restored the religious sense to literature; it has reconsidered the claims of James and Flaubert:

M. Mauriac's first importance to an English reader, therefore, is that he belongs to the company of the great traditional novelists: he is a writer for whom the visible world has not ceased to exist, whose characters have the solidity and importance of men with souls to save or lose, and a writer who claims the traditional and essential right of a novelist, to comment, to express his views. For how tired we have become of the dogmatically "pure" novel, the tradition founded by Flaubert and reaching its magnificent tortuous climax in England in the works of Henry James.[16]

Greene then proceeded to comment on Mauriac's use of the "I":

The exclusion of the author can go too far. Even the author, poor devil, has a right to exist, and M. Mauriac reaffirms that right. It is true that the Flaubertian form is not so completely abandoned in this novel [*La Pharisienne*] as in *Le Baiser au Lepreux:* the "I" of the story plays a part in the action; any commentary there is can be attributed by purists to this fictional "I," but the pretence is thin—"I" is dominated by I. [17]

Greene's own use of the narrator in *The End of the Affair* owes much to the influence of Mauriac. Through Maurice Bendrix, his narrator, Greene makes the secular commentary on the religious action of the novel. But the problem is much more complicated than this: Bendrix, like Charles Ryder in Waugh's *Brideshead Revisited,* is the character on whom the action of the novel leaves the most dominant impression. And like *Brideshead Revisited, The End of the Affair* has adultery for its theme. In Waugh's novel Julia Mottram and Ryder decide that their love is a prelude to a love of God. Ryder's acceptance of the supernatural order in the phenomenal world leads him to a religious conversion. This particular parallel is interesting in the light of Greene's over-all development, for it indicates his coming to a more orthodox approach to the doctrines of the Church. Waugh, who severely criticized the theology of *The Heart of the Matter,* applauded Greene's ability to use the religious theme brilliantly and provokingly in *The End of the Affair:* "Mr. Greene is to be congratulated on a fresh achievement. He shows that in middle life his mind is suppler and his interests wider than in youth; that he is a writer of real stamina. He has triumphantly passed his climacteric where so many talents fail." [18]

Substituting the "advanced" techniques of the contemporary novel for the melodramatic contrivances of the earlier works, Greene attempts to tell the story of a saint. If the reader remembers his assertion that "the greatest saints have been men with more than a normal capacity for evil," the obvious parallels of Mary Magdalene and St. Augustine come to mind. Greene uses the idea of opposites, as he had done in *Brighton Rock,* as the basis of his theme: Hate and love are different sides of the same coin; and, when the coin is set spinning, the differences are impossible to distinguish. Greene's theme is that adultery—lust—can indicate a love of God. "What do we really know of lust?" writes the saintly priest in Georges Bernanos' *The Diary of a Country Priest,* "Lust is a mysterious wound in the side of humanity; or rather at the very source of its life! . . . God! how is it we fail to realize that the mask of pleasure, stripped of all hypocrisy, is that of anguish?" [19]

Maurice Bendrix, a novelist who has not yet committed the crime of becoming popular, writes an account of a love affair that began five or six years earlier. He is uncomfortable in the telling of his story, and Greene suggests the difficulty of the writer in dealing with materials that are part of his own experience. There are rhetorical questions in profusion, contradictions, and apostrophes—all indicating the spiritual turmoil of the writer, who should be objective, betraying himself into subjective analysis. The reader learns a good deal about Bendrix and feels that he is not the most admirable man in the world. Bendrix' account of the affair is the carnal side, the passionate aspect.

After portraying the point of view of the hero, Greene allows the heroine's diary to fall into the lover's hands. In the diary the reader becomes aware of the spiritual struggle which is the chief concern of the novel. A third perspective is achieved through Parkis, a detective whom Bendrix hires to spy on Sarah. A fourth is achieved through Henry Miles, Sarah's husband, the government functionary whose brain Bendrix has been wanting to pick through Sarah. A fifth perspective is achieved through Richard Smythe, a rationalist to whom Sarah goes when she seeks to disbelieve in God. These people are, in effect, the bystanders whom the heroine passes on her journey to sanctity. The parallel with the bystanders of *The Power and the Glory* is obvious.

In their study of Greene, Allott and Farris point out that he had toyed with the idea of portraying the action of *The Heart of the Matter* from the point of view of Louise Scobie but had rejected that idea because it would unnecessarily complicate the pattern of the novel. This indicates, nevertheless, a growing concern with the formulae of both the Jamesian and Conradian novel. The multiplicity of perspective in *The End of the Affair* allows Greene to explore his action from as many avenues as possible. The central conflict is a religious one, and the reader sees it from all its various angles. The other devices—flashback, diary, reverie, letters—throw additional light on the struggle. Greene manipulates these devices so deftly that he succeeds brilliantly in making the religious dilemma the essential concern of the book.

The action of *The End of the Affair* is limited chiefly to an affair between the hero and the heroine; the bystanders emerge as important aspects of the plot only after Sarah's death. Henry Miles, who forms the third corner of one of the two triangles, is important in the struggle because, as Bendrix observes, he has all the cards stacked in his favor: He is Sarah's husband. Bendrix and Sarah meet at a cocktail party, become lovers, and then separate. She dies; and, because her love for God is stronger than her love for a single man, she becomes a saint. It is God who intervenes to make a heroine of Sarah and to put Bendrix on the road to Damascus.

In the light of this situation, it is impossible to agree with those like Norman Shrapnel who, in his review for the *Manchester Guardian,* insists that the few "mild miracles" at the end "can be ignored without much loss." [20] The few minor miracles at the end are the reason for the novel's existence. To deny them is to misunderstand completely Greene's purpose in having written the book. And his purpose is to indicate how adultery can lead to sainthood. The priest at the end of the novel says: " 'There's nothing we can do that the saints haven't done before us.' " [21] Bendrix tells himself: "The saints, one would suppose, in a sense create themselves. They come alive. They are capable of the surprising act or word" (232). Because she loves Bendrix too well, Sarah promises God that she will never see him again if only God will restore him to life, for she believes Bendrix to have been killed in a bomb explosion. To make her keep her promise, God sends His grace in every conceivable way: an unanswered telephone keeps Sarah from talking to Bendrix; a racking cough prevents her kissing him when she does see him; a husband's early return ties her to her home when she has decided to abandon her promise; and death, at the right moment, keeps her from losing all. Sarah succumbs to the grace of God and becomes a saint.

Bendrix, however, at the end of the novel, is doubtful; and he must be, for he maintains the balance between the secular order and the religious order. Yet, the final impression is made upon Bendrix. Because of the flashback technique that Greene uses, the last physical occurrence of the novel's action appears on the first page of the book—Bendrix sits down to tell his story. He speaks of those early days when "we were lucky enough not to believe" (3). Still the novel is Bendrix' journey of exploration, of recognition; and as he writes his and Sarah's story, he comes to a realization of the place of God in the real world. In this way the theme of flight and pursuit is brilliantly incorporated into the writer's creative processes: Bendrix attempts to fly from the grace of God, but God is too persistent a pursuer. The reader learns that Bendrix' spiritual dilemma amounts to an inability "to conceive of any God who is not as simple as a perfect equation, as clear as air" (8). And this had been Major Scobie's problem, just as it had been Péguy's. The convolutions of the novel become the best index to the complexity of the problem of God and His grace in the world.

If Greene relied on *The Waste Land* for the imagery of his earlier novels and entertainments, in *The End of the Affair* he relies as heavily on "Ash Wednesday." Greene's interest in St. John of the Cross is patent—and later, in *The Living Room,* one of his plays, a character reads from St. John. Both Sarah and Bendrix, within broad outline, follow the pattern of spiritual awareness described in St. John's *La Noce Oscura.* Here St. John describes the individual soul entering into a period of purgation, and he describes the battle between the spirit and the senses. (Eliot's demon of the stair is one of St. John of the Cross's many contributions to "Ash Wednesday.") St. John describes, as does Eliot, the penitent experiencing despair, rebellion, and drought in his ascent to heaven. He speaks constantly of love, the interceding factor in helping man on his way to God. And St. John does not minimize the influence of the senses. Like Eliot, Greene makes conscious use of this symbolism, particularly that of the stair. In her journal Sarah describes a dream:

Two days ago I had such a sense of peace and quiet and love. Life was going to be happy again, but last night I dreamed I was walking up a long staircase to meet Maurice at the top. I was still happy because when I reached the top of the staircase we were going to make love. I called to him that I was coming, but it wasn't Maurice's voice who answered; it was like a stranger's that boomed like a foghorn warning lost ships, and scared me. I thought, he's left his flat and gone away and I don't know where he is, and going down the stairs again the water rose beyond my waist and the hall was thick with mist. (151)

When Bendrix first meets Sarah, he is not impressed by her because, paradoxically, she is beautiful. To love, Bendrix must feel himself superior, chiefly because he has one leg shorter than the other, a handicap that accounts for a good deal of his cynicism. Contrary to all his convictions, he falls in love with Sarah, and their affair progresses splendidly. But Bendrix is jealous of Sarah —of her husband and of her life away from him; he fears that one day she will cease to love him. There are violent arguments and equally violent reconciliations.

Sarah refuses to speak of the permanence of their love when Bendrix encourages her to do so. Yet she often surprises him by telling him that she loves him more than any man she has ever known. At this period of her life, there is nothing of the saint in Sarah; there is no thought of God in her promiscuous life. There had been other men before Bendrix, and he reasons that there will be others after him. She finds in him the lover her husband has never been. When she tells Bendrix that she never loved anybody or anything as she does him, she does not realize that this "perfect" human relationship is a shadow of a greater love. In her complete abandonment to her lover she reckons only on the gratification of her physical passions; she does not realize the emptiness of her spiritual self.

Having experienced perfect human love with Bendrix, Sarah renounces him for God, and nothing short of divine love will satisfy her. Unconsciously she has made provision for God in her affair, for she has always avoided calling Bendrix by his Christian name, always referring to him as "you." Just as the "I" of Bendrix indicates the commentary on the spiritual theme, the "you," in its ambiguity is expressive of God. It is, therefore, the unseen presence of God that hovers over the adulterous bed and informs the physical love of Sarah and Maurice. Again Greene's audacity is unbelievable; it is more so because he succeeds in making his thesis believable. The unseen "you" makes jealousy and anger the tools of His grace. God is the "third man" whom Bendrix engages Parkis to find. Again the theme of God's pursuit is put to use.

When the novel begins, Bendrix tells his reader how he ran into Henry Miles one rainy night. Henry does not know that Bendrix and Sarah have been lovers; and he, Henry, confides to Bendrix that he feels Sarah is unfaithful. Bendrix' hatred and jealousy flare again even though he has had no contact with Sarah for several years. Bendrix agrees with Henry to the advisability of hiring a detective, and he volunteers to relieve Henry of the anxiety by making the arrangements himself. But Henry decides that such a plan is a discredit to him. Then acknowledging for the first time Bendrix' enthusiasm, he discovers that Sarah had been his confidant's mistress.

Without Henry's knowledge Bendrix hires Parkis, a good-natured, inept detective reminiscent of Jones in *The Ministry of Fear,* to discover Sarah's affair. The theme of flight and pursuit finds its expression on a spiritual level in Sarah's evasion of Bendrix and of God, as well as in Bendrix' evasion. Somehow Parkis manages to secure Sarah's journal—she never suspects that so intimate an account of her life is gone—and Bendrix discovers why she called an end to the affair. He reads her description of that day when, together in bed, the bombs began to fall. Looking to see whether or not the landlady had gone down to the shelter, Bendrix had been knocked unconscious. Finding him in the hall, Sarah believed him dead; she returned to the bedroom and prayed:

Dear God, I said—why dear?—make me believe. I can't believe. Make me. I said, I'm a bitch and a fake and I hate myself. I can't do anything of myself. *Make* me believe. I shut my eyes tight, and I pressed my nails into the palms of my hands until I could feel nothing but the pain, and I said, I *will* believe. Give him a chance. Let him have his happiness. Do this, and I'll believe. But that wasn't enough. It doesn't hurt to believe. So I said, I love him and I'll do anything if You'll make him alive. I said very slowly, I'll give him up forever, only let him be alive with a chance, and I pressed and pressed and I could feel the skin break, and I said, people can love without seeing each other, can't they, they love You all their lives without seeing You, and then he came in at the door, and he was alive, and I thought now the agony of being without him starts, and I wished he was safely back dead again under the door.   (116-17)

Bendrix discovers that a third corner of an unsuspected, or spiritual, triangle is God; He had been the silent witness to all their acts of sex and had intervened to claim Sarah for His own. God had accepted her promise and had taken Sarah at her word. He *makes* her believe, for Sarah chooses heaven as surely as Pinkie Brown in *Brighton Rock* chooses hell. Once Bendrix learns of Sarah's love for God, he transfers to Him the hate he has felt for Sarah. But he had hated her only because he loved her. Now, with all the strength of his love, he hates God, his rival.

[110]

Sarah's promise never to see Bendrix again causes her to start on the long climb to heaven. Trying to avoid the implications of her promise, she seeks solace in other men; but all that she experiences is a sense of dryness. In the early stages of her spiritual awareness Sarah feels that she doesn't believe in God. But she does believe. Since physical love no longer affords any pleasure, she knows that she cannot hurt God that way. Luckily, she does not think of suicide as Major Scobie does. Sarah knows that God exists, since He put the thought of the vow in her mind; but she hates Him. Her hate is, paradoxically, the statement of her love—she has yet to learn to put her trust in God. And this she cannot do until she acknowledges the fact that by betraying her out of physical life, He has shown her the way to spiritual life. In her early rebellion Sarah feels that she can leave the desert whenever she wants to: " 'I can catch a train home tomorrow and ring him [Bendrix] up on the telephone . . . and we can spend the night together' " (114). But she knows this is impossible. Sarah has an overwhelming desire to love, but she doesn't know what to do with it.

The alternating spasms of love and hate she feels for both God and Bendrix eventually bring her to an understanding of her real love. She admits that what she had felt for Bendrix was merely a prelude to the love she feels for God:

Did I ever love Maurice as much before I loved You? Or was it You I really loved all the time? Did I touch You when I touched him? Could I have touched You if I hadn't touched him first, touched him as I never touched Henry, anybody? And he loved me and touched me as he never did it with any other woman. But was it me he loved, or You? For he hated in me the things You hate. He was on your side all the time without knowing it. You willed our separation, but he willed it too. He worked for it with his anger and his jealousy, and he worked for it with his love. For he gave me so much love and I gave him so much love that soon there wasn't anything left when we'd finished but You. (150-51)

This is the key passage to the understanding of the novel, for it states the theme. In her love for Bendrix, Sarah finds love for God. And the preparation is made for Bendrix' own orientation into the scheme of God. In learning to love God, Sarah finds peace. And this peace Sarah leaves to Bendrix as her legacy.

She writes in her journal: "When I ask You for pain, You give me peace. Give it to him too. Give him my peace—he needs it more" (151). Again Green echoes Eliot's "Ash Wednesday" as Sarah prays for strength and asks for peace.

Sarah's suffering teaches her not only to believe in God, to love Him, but to have faith in Him. Her faith is her trust, and it is as firm as that of the greatest saints. In the letter she writes to Bendrix, she says: "I believe there's a God—I believe the whole bag of tricks; there's nothing I don't believe; they could subdivide the Trinity into a dozen parts and I'd believe. They could dig up records that Christ had been invented by Pilate to get himself promoted and I'd believe just the same. I've caught belief like a disease. I've fallen into belief like I fell in love. . . . I fought belief for longer than I fought love, but I haven't any fight left" (182).

In her flight from Bendrix and from God, Sarah had stumbled into a Catholic Church and she had determined to become a member of it. Henry and Bendrix, who find a common bond in their love for Sarah, decide against a Catholic burial. There is no record of Sarah's ever having been baptized, and Bendrix refuses to permit Henry to make the arrangements which would have pleased Sarah most. For Bendrix is determined to hate Sarah's God for having deprived him of her. One remembers how bitterly he had hated Sarah only a few weeks before. The pattern begins anew: Sarah hated God for making her keep her vow; now Bendrix hates because he must. The Catholic priest who enters into the action of the novel at the last minute, in typical Greene fashion, sets about his job of asserting the norm of the Church. He argues against cremation at Golder's Green, but Bendrix, in his hate, is firm in wanting to inflict a pagan burial on Sarah. "I wanted her burned up," he writes, "I wanted to be able to say, Resurrect that body if you can; my jealousy has not finished, like Henry's, with her death. It was as if she were alive still, in the company of a lover she had preferred to me" (170).

The day of the funeral Bendrix meets by appointment Waterbury, a writer of reviews. He takes an instinctive dislike to the young man and takes his girl away from him. Bendrix knows that he cannot love the girl, but he insists on proving his masculine superiority to the reviewer. What Bendrix really wants is to show Sarah that he can get along without her, but he realizes the futility of his gesture. He implores Sarah in prayer to get him out of his predicament, not for his sake but for that of the girl. Conveniently, Sarah's mother comes on the scene, and Bendrix wonders whether it is coincidence or an answer to his prayer that has brought Mrs. Bertram along. From her he learns that Sarah has been a Roman Catholic all her life, that she had been baptized at the age of two. The sainthood of Sarah becomes surer and surer, and the Roman Catholicism of the heroine becomes, indeed, much like the Fatality that hangs over Major Scobie. It is the frame of reference that gives meaning to the narrative.

The "miracles" begin to accrue. Lance, Parkis' son, ill with appendicitis, asks his father for the gift that Sarah had promised him. Parkis secures an old child's book from Henry, and Lance dreams that night that Sarah touches him on the side and cures him of his pain. Bendrix thinks about the coincidence, but he dismisses the idea of miracle. As the representative of the secular order, he is well within his rights to do so. Nevertheless, he cannot help but remember the priest's comment to Henry: " 'It only goes to show what a good woman your wife was' " (225).

In her flight from grace Sarah had gone to Richard Smythe, a rationalist, who in true nineteenth-century fashion preached of the impossibility of belief in God. Smythe spoke to Sarah of the confusion implicit in the gospel texts, of Christ's never claiming to be God, and of chaos in the world. To keep from believing in God, Sarah had sought the proofs that would deny His existence; but each "proof" had made her feel more strongly within herself the truth of God's reality. Smythe's face, marred by a birthmark, had touched her pity. She loved Smythe because of his unhappiness, and she realized that his rebellion against God was induced by the physical defect. Here the theme of pity is brilliantly associated with the sense of God and the humility of the saint. When Bendrix runs into Smythe several days after the funeral, he discovers that the strawberry mark has disappeared from Smythe's face. Smythe first tells Bendrix that he has been treated electrically; later, over the telephone, he admits that the mark had disappeared of itself, and Bendrix remembers that Sarah had recorded in her journal how she had kissed it. He knows that such disfigurements are often hysterical in origin and that they can be reasoned away by psychiatric treatment; but this time he cannot dismiss the idea of a miracle so easily.

As far as the structure of the novel is concerned, these "miracles" or "coincidences" at the end cannot be summarily put aside. Since Greene works consciously with the anatomy of sainthood and since the precedent of sinners being the preferred of God has been set by such luminaries as St. Augustine and Mary Magdalene, the reader must accept the fact that Greene wishes the coincidences to be considered as miracles. To all intents and purposes, Sarah Miles is a saint, and the next steps in her spiritual recognition are beatification, then canonization. But it will never come to this because Bendrix, in his hate, refuses to allow the facts to be vulgarized. As the representative of the world in general, Bendrix' "rational" approach to the dilemma is the only possible one.

The novel ostensibly ends on a note of perplexity. Bendrix finds himself in the center of indifference, on the rim of the everlasting yes. He is dominated by hatred, but he knows that hate is the opposite side of love's coin: "All right, have it your way, I said to Sarah. I believe you live and that He exists, but it will take more than your prayers to turn this hatred of Him into love. He robbed me, and . . . I'll rob Him of what He wants in me. I can't be cured like Smythe or Parkis's boy. Hatred is in my brain, not in my stomach or my skin. It can't be removed like a strawberry mark or an ache. Didn't I hate you as well as love you? And don't I hate myself?" (239). Capable of a great hate, Bendrix is now capable of a great love; and the reader cannot believe that he is too old to learn to love. Somehow, the Blessed Damozel is leaning over the golden bar of heaven yearning for him, and he has just begun to learn.

Technically, *The End of the Affair* is brilliant. Greene's use of the diary and of the journal allows him not only to characterize his people but also to portray various levels of meaning concerning the spiritual drama enacted. Bendrix looks at Sarah; Sarah looks at herself as she looks at God. The bystanders look at Sarah, and she leaves her mark on them. The dream sequences allow Greene to describe in symbolic terms the conflict within her, and the debates allow him to give concrete expression to her struggle. The flashbacks permit him to show the reader the various phases of the development of the action and to portray the state of Bendrix' mind as he describes the affair.

The End of the Affair is, furthermore, the most Catholic of

Greene's novels, in the narrow sense. Even Waugh complains that the novel is, perhaps, too sectarian, since it implies that the Church is like a secret society. Greene's previous stories had ended with the death of the central characters and had permitted the priest to reestablish the norm of the Church after men had finished wrestling with their souls. In *The End of the Affair*, however, the theme of sainthood is so obviously Roman Catholic in its development that the importance of the priest is negligible. Furthermore, his role is minimized by the fact that the melodramatic framework has all but disappeared. It is, nevertheless, to Greene's credit that he has been able to take a cliché situation and transfuse it with spiritual life.

Melodrama had afforded Greene the best opportunity to portray a spiritual theme allegorically in *Brighton Rock*. In *The End of the Affair*, however, there is little or no need to allegorize. In *The Heart of the Matter* the Roman Catholicism of Major Scobie had hung over the British sector of Africa like fatality. The reader had appreciated the dramatic structure of the novel and had been able to sympathize with a hero whose salvation had wisely been left undetermined. In *The End of the Affair*, however, Greene moves away from melodrama into a broader dimension as he comes closer to the novel that Mauriac defines in his works. Mauriac makes use of the modern devices of novel writing, and Greene must try his hand at these before going on to create characters who approximate in their own idiom the complex individuals that dominate Mauriac's Bordeaux country. As a result, Greene's technique becomes more realistic.

This is Greene's triumph: He has been steadily and surely improving his art. Since *Brighton Rock*, he has developed the scope of the novel in England; he has devoted more and more energy to characterization and less and less to the contrivances of plot. The religious theme has been more and more artistically integrated into the over-all pattern of the novels until, in *The End of the Affair*, it has become one with the plot. By using devices such as the diary, the dream, the reverie, and the debate, Greene gives symbolic unity to his work while characterizing his people. The spiritual dryness and the symbol of the stair which Sarah describes in her journal are expressive of this ability. Nevertheless, in *The End of the Affair*—as in *The Power and the Glory*—

Greene reasserts the value of love. Perhaps the greatest miracle of all is that he brings Henry Miles and Bendrix, the chief by-standers, to a closer understanding of one another.

V The Quiet American

Although *The Quiet American* pays lip service to the philosophy of Existentialism, the novel is in reality a further elaboration of the same theme that informed *The Ministry of Fear* and *The Heart of the Matter*. Set in Indochina, *The Quiet American*—like *The Heart of the Matter* before it—compresses the political issues into the differences that exist among human beings. The ideologies of Alden Pyle, the quiet American; of General Thé, the exponent and head of the cult of power mysteriously referred to as the Third Force; of Vigot, the disinterested French administrator of justice who reads Pascal; of Heng, the Communist, who forces Fowler to "engage" or to take sides if only "to remain human"—all these are dramatized in the relationships that ultimately form the meaning of the novel. For, although the background is political and although the French Existentialist philosophy goes a long way toward explaining the anti-Americanism of the book, *The Quiet American* is primarily about human beings involved in an ethical dilemma.

Existentialism insists on the cult of the individual—on what Sartre calls "le culte du moi." One branch of Existentialism, Sartre's, denies God and makes atheism the reigning philosophy governing individual conduct. Greene, of course, could not be considered as advocating this aspect of the philosophy. Under the branch of Catholic Existentialism, as defined by the philosopher Marcel, God is somehow, and for many rather mysteriously, accepted. But, strangely, it seems that it is Sartrian Existentialism that best defines Greene's approach to Fowler in *The Quiet American*.

At the heart of Sartrian Existentialism lies the point that has attracted Greene, who is always the champion of the individual. This point is the individual's freedom of choice, or his "engagement." The vital force of Sartre's Existentialism is how it demonstrates the essential and indefinable character of man; this demonstration often produces anguish, "angoisse." For Sartre only a dead man (and here Pyle might be considered) can be judged, for he alone is "defined"; he alone has finished forming himself.

Only the dead man has achieved totalization of his experience and his existence. The living man may evade responsibility, paradoxically "creating" himself as he exercises this freedom. But the moment of choice, of engagement, must at last come if the individual is to achieve existence; and the moment of choice, of engagement, may, and in Sartre's novels frequently does, bring death.[22]

In *The Quiet American,* as in classical drama, the sense of history is dynamically superimposed on the actions of those who go about the business of life. The city of Saigon becomes a microcosm that reflects much of twentieth-century political thinking. *The Quiet American* is the one major Greene novel that does not directly make use of a Roman Catholic background, although Fowler's estranged wife and Vigot, the inspector of police, are both Catholics. Fowler, a middle-aged newspaper reporter—he resents the term "journalist" because it implies a commitment to the world that he feels he cannot make—is nominally an atheist, although several times he addresses himself to the God in whom he does not believe. Aided in his occupation by Dominguez, an enigmatic Moslem who has the ability to discern the germ of truth in the mystifying reports of offensives and counter-offensives that inundate the city, Fowler lives with Phuong, his beautiful mistress, enjoying his opium pipe and placidly but cynically his existence. Into the "uncommitted" pattern of his life comes Alden Pyle—American, aged thirty-two, Harvard-nurtured, innocent, and full of intellectual idealism and enthusiasm. Fowler and Pyle respect and have a reciprocal understanding of each other's basic integrity and goodness, but neither can be referred to as sinless.

Criticized by American reviewers for its supposed anti-Americanism, *The Quiet American* has been misunderstood because of and in spite of the ironic commentary Greene makes concerning Pyle's commitment to democracy and to action: "He was young and ignorant and silly and he got involved. He had no more of a notion than any of you what the whole affair's about. . . . He never saw anything he hadn't heard in a lecture hall, and his writers and his lecturers made a fool of him. When he saw a dead body he couldn't even see the wounds. A Red menace, a soldier of democracy." [23]

The point that has been neglected is essentially the core of the novel's meaning. What Greene intends to depict in the course of the novel's activity is that idealism, when uninformed by experience, is a dangerous weapon in a world coerced by the cult of power, symbolized by General Thé and his mysterious Third Force. Greene wishes, moreover, to satirize the belief that money alone can secure peace and understanding. The poem from which Fowler reads as he betrays Pyle is Arthur Clough's "Dipsychus," the twin-souled; and its satiric refrain, the reader will remember, is "So pleasant it is to have money, heigh ho!" (234). Equally important, Greene wishes to describe the cowardice implicit in living an "uncommitted" life in a world on the brink of destruction.

To fulfill his thematic intent, Greene employs the innocent Alden Pyle, who is symbolically the opposite of Henry James's innocent, the American sent to a decadent Europe to reestablish the importance of the human act. Greene's innocent—Pyle—is a leaven that brings about bloodshed and tragedy, because his innocence is inadequate in a world corrupted by the experience of evil. Pyle is compared to a "dumb leper who has lost his bell, wandering the world, meaning no harm" (40), and as a hero in a boy's adventure story who is impregnably armored by good intentions and ignorance; indeed he derives from Anthony Farrant of *England Made Me*. In this respect Pyle is like his country. "I wish sometimes you had a few bad motives," Fowler says to him, "you might understand a little more about human beings. And that applies to your country too . . ." (173). However, Greene comments as ironically about Fowler's position as he does about Pyle's; both men are aspects of goodness, and much of the novel's meaning centers on the genuine friendship that develops between the two. "You cannot love with intuition" (13), says Fowler; and later he asks: "Am I the only one who really cared for Pyle?" (19). Fowler's idealism is informed by experience; Pyle's, by innocence.

The pawn in this game of experience versus innocence is Phuong, whose name means phoenix. In the plot she represents both the enigma of the East and the desire of the East for political status. Her allegiance to Fowler is neither romantic nor materialistic; she is not, however, incapable of loyalty. She leaves Fowler and attaches herself to Pyle—"youth and hope and seriousness," —who promises her the status she seeks. But ironically this to him is Boston—conformity to American social patterns—and he fails her more than "age and despair" (14). What Fowler offers her is the understanding of experience and the tenderness of his kindly cynicism. At the novel's end, after his betrayal of Pyle to the Communists, Fowler is able to offer her the marriage she desires, for his wife agrees in a moment of generosity to give him a divorce despite her Roman Catholic scruples.

Although *The Quiet American* fits neatly into the Existentialist pattern, the philosophy that animates the character of Fowler is the same as that which decides the activities of Arthur Rowe in *The Ministry of Fear* and of Major Scobie in *The Heart of the Matter*. Stripped of Rowe's sentimentalism and of Scobie's religious preoccupations, Fowler seems less noble than his predecessors; but he is, nevertheless, propelled by the same compassion. Again this pity is visualized as a form of egotism when Fowler says: "I know myself and I know the depth of my selfishness. I cannot be at ease (and to be at ease is my chief wish) if someone else is in pain, visibly or audibly or tactually. Sometimes this is mistaken by the innocent for unselfishness, when all I am doing is sacrificing a small good . . . for the sake of a far greater good, a peace of mind, when I need think only of myself" (146-47).

Fowler is, furthermore, the most Conradian of Greene's heroes, and there is a curious parallel to *Victory* to be seen in the novel. Although Fowler and Heyst are separated by years of political and social change, they are both fundamentally unengaged souls. Each avoids entrapments and each egotistically shuns commitment—Heyst because of early training, and Fowler because of the disappointments of experience. And yet both are made aware of the importance of the human act, and each makes a choice— Heyst for life which, paradoxically, brings about his death, and Fowler for death which, ironically, commits him to life. Fowler is trapped by his pity for suffering, first when he sees the dead guard at the outpost, then when he sees the dead child after Pyle's diolacton bomb explodes in the square. Fowler realizes that innocence in a ravaged world amounts to pain and suffering that can be counted as dead bodies and mutilated children. After the crucial meeting with Granger, an incident that has been much admired but little understood, Fowler realizes his affinity to Pyle; and he asks, "Must I too have my foot thrust in the mess of life before I saw the pain?" (245). He goes into the street without hope to find Phuong, who waits vainly for the dead Pyle. Fowler has taken sides to remain human, and the realization of his compassionate spirit overwhelms him. The novel ends with the sentence, "Everything had gone right with me since he died, but how I wished there existed someone to whom I could say that I was sorry" (249). And the irony needs no comment.

Although *The Quiet American* makes little mention of religious matters, there is in the shadows the same religious feeling that infiltrates the entertainments and justifies their ethics. Although Fowler does not believe in God, he nevertheless addresses Him. He leaves Pyle's death not to chance, or to Fate, but to God; and at the novel's end, he wishes there were someone to whom he could say that he was sorry. The statement is tentative, and the reader interprets it as Greene would have him do. What Fowler is searching for is permanence. "From childhood on I had never believed in permanence," he says, "and yet I longed for it. I was afraid of losing happiness" (50). The religious sense is also reinforced by the nature of Pyle's death. He does not die from the knife wounds that the Communists inflict upon him; instead, he drowns. The scapegoat motif and the drowned man motif and the Judas motif add the religious note that helps explain Greene's meaning.

VI A Burnt-Out Case

In the journal that Greene kept while traveling in the Belgian Congo, he records how in January, 1959, he began his journey "with a novel already beginning to form in my head by way of a situation—a stranger who turns up in a remote leper-colony." [24] *In Search of a Character* indicates Greene's approach to the problems of novel writing and also makes the point that his characters shape themselves within the situation to emerge from the pages as unique and sometimes terrifying individuals. In other words, *In Search of a Character* is another proof that Greene does not approach his craft from the point of view of the dilettante Christian theologist. Indeed, for the dilettante theologian Greene has little more than contempt, and Rycker in *A Burnt-Out Case* is an example of this attitude.

The journal includes Greene's notes on the incidence and the varieties of leprosy; it records his observations on leprophobes and leprophiles, and it suggests his compassion for the lepers themselves, their social and domestic difficulties. The journal also records his genuine admiration for the nuns and priests who care for the ills of the body before worrying about the nature of sin and grace among the lepers; it suggests Greene's affection for those who dedicate their lives to the care of the afflicted. It is no wonder then that Doctor Colin in *A Burnt-Out Case* refused to take shape as Greene had at first anticipated. So strong is Greene's feeling for Colin that the doctor at the novel's end assumes the responsibility that Father Rank in *The Heart of the Matter* and the priest in *Brighton Rock* are accorded—he makes the final, choric commentary on the story's action; he restores, therefore, a sane and normal perspective to the little world of the leper colony.

The journal further describes—perhaps this is its chief interest —the emergence of the character who came to be called Querry, his name suggestive of his search and longing. It records the character's transition from an Englishman who knew no French to a half-Englishman with a thorough competence in French because of his Belgian parent, his occupation as an architect, and his successes both vocational and amatory. As pointed out above, the journal also testifies to Greene's concern with his craft—his nervousness over a correct beginning; his fear that he might over-plot, tell a "good" story; his worry over the credibility of the situations; and his concern over transitions. In short, the journal includes the numerous observations, hesitations, starts, and stops that go into the composition of a novel. Although not so detailed as *The Lawless Roads, In Search of a Character* is indispensable in a consideration of Greene's artistry, not only because it points out that Greene is not a dogmatist, but also that he is a writer of great talent whose Catholicism may not be conveniently overlooked like a bad case of psoriasis. In the Introduction, Greene says that the task of writing *A Burnt-Out Case* proved so difficult that he feels that the effort of another full-length novel is beyond him—a feeling that one hopes will pass when the situation for another presents itself.

Published in 1961, *A Burnt-Out Case* reflects the same serious tone that characterizes *The Power and the Glory, The Heart of the Matter,* and *The End of the Affair.* And like these novels, *A Burnt-Out Case,* set in a leper colony in Africa, makes use of background for effect and for symbolic value; but the emphasis falls—as it does in all of Greene's major works—on the relationship between character and event.

An architect of international reputation and a successful and notorious lover, Querry makes his way hundreds of miles up one of the Congo's tributaries to a leprosarium. "Are you stopping here?" asks Colin, the physician who treats the lepers. To which Querry replies, "The boat goes no further." [25] The resemblance to Conrad's *Heart of Darkness* is apparent, but the mysteries are indeed different. In *In Search of a Character* Greene says of Conrad's story, "It is as if Conrad had taken an episode in his own life and tried to lend it, for the sake of 'literature,' a greater significance than it will hold" (33). In *A Burnt-Out Case* Greene also grapples with this problem. He says, "This is not a *roman à clef*, but an attempt to give dramatic expression to various types of belief, half-belief, and non-belief, in the kind of setting, removed from world-politics and household-preoccupations, where such differences are felt acutely and find expression" (vii). He struggles to keep the "episode" from assuming greater significance than it will hold. Again, he approaches myth.

Querry is a Roman Catholic who has gone beyond feeling. He does not know what he is looking for; nor, he says, does he care. Long before his journey to Africa he had come to the limit of his spiritual resources. A man to whom success as an ecclesiastical architect had come too easily, he had grown dissatisfied, his art frivolous; ironically the decline had been noticed by none but himself. The world had gone on acclaiming him until his head "callused with pride and success" admitted that his faith, his vocation, even his love-making, were sham: "'He had believed that quite sincerely when he loved his work he was loving the King and that when he made love to a woman he was at least imitating in a faulty way the King's love for his people'" (197).

With the discovery that he could no longer believe in God, whose existence he had once proved by "historical, logical, philosophical, and etymological methods," Querry accepted the fact that his work had been done for love of himself (192). Nevertheless, and this is the novel's point—"types of belief, half-belief, and non-belief"—Querry wonders if his non-belief is after all nothing but a final and conclusive proof of God's existence. At the novel's end Dr. Colin says, "You're too troubled by your lack of faith, Querry. You keep on fingering it like a sore you want to get rid of" (239).

Perhaps Querry is seeking a return to usefulness and integrity. The doctor and the priests teach him much about genuine compassion and understanding; the lepers teach him much about suffering and unhappiness. Deo Gratias, Querry's servant is a burnt-out case—one in whom the disease has run its course, having eroded in this instance all the fingers and toes. He and Querry come to parallel one another: Querry's spiritual mutilation matches Deo Gratias' physical handicap. Querry's search for usefulness is symbolized by Pendelé, a place of contentment that Deo Gratias remembers from childhood. Pendelé, neither the Christian heaven nor a pagan sanctuary, becomes for Querry a reason for living—usefulness, innocence perhaps, an escape from success and the demands of the ego, contentment. Paradoxically, it is Querry's reawakening interest in human suffering, the rebirth perhaps of his pity, that keeps him from finding Pendelé and ultimately brings about his death. By the novel's end Querry is pronounced cured of the disease that has left him symbolically a burnt-out case; Dr. Colin says: "He'd learned to serve other people, you see, and to laugh. An odd laugh, but it was a laugh all the same" (247). The reader remembers how often Querry had accepted Colin's prognoses.

The keynote of the novel is ambiguity: the mystery that Querry arouses as he moves against the lepers, the priests, the French and English colonials, the government officials. Greene says in his notes for the novel, ". . . I feel that X must die because an element of insoluble mystery has to remain" (38). The means that Greene chooses to dispatch Querry is one that he used many times before, the triangle. Querry becomes innocently involved with Rycker and his childlike wife, and is killed by the jealous husband. But despite the triangle relationship, *A Burnt-Out Case* does not record—as Orville Prescott insists in his review of the novel in *The New York Times*—Greene's "curious conviction that sexual guilt is the beginning of wisdom and that adultery is one of the better paths toward grace." [26] Indeed Querry feels no guilt for his sexual promiscuity. Prescott, it seems, is reading *A Burnt-Out Case* in the light of *The End of the Affair* and *The Heart of the Matter,* in which novels the problem of adultery is indeed important. For Prescott goes on to say, "The subtleties of religious dogmas have never been very tractable for fiction. Novels steeped in eroticism and largely preoccupied with sins of the flesh are a poor media for the dramatization of problems of faith." [27]

"Eroticism" and "dogma" hardly seem suitable keywords for *A Burnt-Out Case*. Rather it is what Querry represents to others that forms the heart of the novel and lends it its "mystery." To Rycker, the *colon*, he is the Catholic architect, versed in dogma and knowledgeable in theological matters. Rycker seeks consolation for lechery and pride, but Querry is too shrewd to allow himself to be persuaded that Rycker's squalid egotism is anything more. To Father Thomas, Querry is a living hero, perhaps an embryonic saint. ". . . [D]on't let's recognize them before the Church does. We shall be saved a lot of disappointment that way," says the superior (105). To the majority of the priests and to Dr. Colin, Querry is a man seeking a place for himself in the world of men and, to some, in the eyes of God. To Parkinson, the journalist, he is "good copy." Querry recognizes in him, just as Scobie recognizes in Yusef, the degradation and decay that is in himself. The motif is from Dostoevski.

To Mme. Rycker, Querry is escape from the tedium of African plantation life and the intolerable concupiscence of her marriage. It is her naïveté—Querry spends an innocent night with her in a hotel—that leads to the denouement of the novel and to Querry's death. The situation is, however, difficult to credit; it occasions, therefore, the chief shortcoming of the novel. The fact that the irony is so apparent—Querry's affair, no affair at all—makes the scene difficult to accept. Querry, who seeks above all to safeguard the precarious peace that he is slowly finding at the leprosarium, is too old a hand to be caught by such a feminine wile.

A Burnt-Out Case is not Greene's best novel, but it is a fine piece of writing and a truly exciting story. It indicates, as do the other novels, that Greene is a novelist who does not use just one religious stance but a variety of stances; these are dictated not by dogma but by what the novelist has chosen to face in "this" novel. His works contrast greatly with the dogmatic Marxian novel—as he himself has pointed out in the exchange of letters, cited earlier in this study, with Elizabeth Bowen and V. S. Pritchett. The Marxian novel offers judgments that are much more in the cards at the outset. In the final analysis, what Greene does is to make a case for Christianity, not just for Roman Catholic dogma, on aesthetic grounds. To insist on his Roman Catholicism is to misunderstand his Christian humanism and to lose sight of his artistry.

CHAPTER 6

The Drama

MUCH critical attention has been given to Graham Greene as a novelist who deals with the theme of sin and damnation in his major works, and such novels as *Brighton Rock, The Heart of the Matter, The Power and the Glory,* and *The End of the Affair* have gained for him a sizable literary reputation. Nevertheless, a great many of Greene's admirers cling to the belief that the best of Greene is still to be found in his early thrillers: *A Gun For Sale, The Confidential Agent,* and *The Ministry of Fear.* Add to this that all save one or two of his works have been translated into the motion picture form, *The Third Man* and more recently *Our Man from Havana* gaining immense popular success, and one finds a writer of "many parts." Comparatively little attention, however, has been given to Greene the dramatist, despite the fact that he has written three plays, all of which have received critical as well as popular acclaim in both the United States and England.

These ventures into drama are not surprising when one remembers that Greene was very much preoccupied with dramatic presentations in several of his later novels, especially in *The Power and the Glory* and *The Quiet American.* Perhaps it needs to be pointed out once more that Greene's apprenticeship as film critic on the *Spectator* and his knowledge of cinematographic techniques and tricks of suspense contributed to his sense of melodrama apparent in his early novels and entertainments. In the later novels, however, his themes have been developed with a careful eye for dramatic possibilities engendered in and by the action: in *The Power and the Glory,* for example, the main theme —the power of God versus the power of a godless state—is ironically developed in the dramatic debate between the whiskey priest and the lieutenant of the new order.

The Drama

Greene's dramas are interesting because they add to the theater a dimension which might be termed religio-philosophical dilemma. In two of his plays, *The Living Room* (1953) and *The Potting Shed* (1957), Greene seems to be recapitulating favorite themes; and an analysis of certain changes and modifications serves to determine Greene's range as a creative artist. The third of his plays, *The Complaisant Lover* (1959), stands in relation to *The Living Room* and *The Potting Shed* much as *Our Man in Havana* relates to the novels and its predecessor entertainments. This play is a brisk, witty, oftentimes farcical treatment of the triangle situation Greene had used in several of his novels, as well as in *The Living Room*. But where the emphasis in the novels and in *The Living Room* falls on the emotional and spiritual complications of characters involved in basically tragic situations, in *The Complaisant Lover* it falls on the comic involvements of a domestic tragedy. The second Mrs. Tanqueray, Candida, and the Constant Wife are in the wings, contributing to the hilarity and underscoring the ironical treatment of the theme.

I The Living Room

The Living Room uses for its situation the triangle relationship that has characterized many of the major novels since *The Heart of The Matter*. As in that novel, the religious theme of the play insists on a character's inability to conceive of a kindly and understanding God; and the major conflict of the play becomes that of the individual against the orthodox religious conception of God as defined by the Roman Catholic Church. But once again Greene is not primarily interested in defining the beliefs of his Church, but in describing a dilemma in which human beings are forced into an emotional *cul de sac;* to ask of either *The Living Room* or *The Potting Shed* an answer to the religious problems posed by the plays is to misunderstand completely Greene's intention. Greene is above all concerned with individuals, and it is this concern that makes him one of the best, most vital of writers at work today. The characters in his novels and in his plays make a place for themselves in an experience of life which, ultimately, they control.

Peter Glenville, the British producer of *The Living Room,* points out in the Introduction to the 1957 William Heinemann edition that the play was difficult and unexpected both in theme and manner. He goes on to characterize it as a drama full of mood and challenge, elusive and yet passionate with conviction; as a drama that borrowed nothing from stock theatrical convention, and one whose meaning was to be discovered through style, rhythm, and imaginative concentration on the essentials of character:

The majority of English plays are romantically conceived, and their absence of intellectual vitality is compensated for by a warm optimism in the emotional pattern. In this play there is a firm and masculine optimism in the matter of intellectual conviction, combined with a searing pessimism that concerns the question of immediate satisfaction of emotional needs. Moreover it is written within the framework and premise of Catholic belief. This play is no apologia for Catholicism. . . . The play is not for or against Catholics, it is about them—or rather about certain individual Catholics who find themselves (through their own fault) in a terrible dilemma. . . .[1]

In other words, the reader need not concern himself with the tenets of Catholicism except as they reflect upon the actions of the characters who find themselves involved in an experience of life that seems to admit no earthly solution.

The Living Room concerns Rose Pemberton's coming to live with her great aunts after the death of her mother. The aunts, Teresa and Helen Browne (their names are perhaps allusions to Teresa, the Little Flower, and to Helena, the determined mother of Constantine) are intensely and narrowly Roman Catholic. Although she has been brought up a Roman Catholic, Rose is not fanatical in her devotion; her father was, after all, not a Catholic. Teresa and Helen care for their brother James, a priest unable to continue in his office because of an accident to his legs. Like Father Rank in *The Heart of the Matter,* James feels keenly his limitations when called upon to assist the suffering. Although she is the younger of the two sisters, Helen is the stronger willed. And when she discovers that Rose is having an affair with Michael Dennis, the middle-aged executor of her estate, she cruelly induces Teresa to fall ill, thereby making an appeal to Rose's pity and keeping her from running off with Michael. Helen reasons that it is better for Rose to conduct an affair and remain within the Church and the framework of its forgiveness than to cut herself off completely from repentance by living an adulterous life as Michael's common-law wife.

[128]

Michael Dennis is married to a neurotic wife who resembles Mrs. Fellows, Coral's mother, in *The Power and the Glory* and Louise Scobie in *The Heart of the Matter*. The three women have in common the early deaths of their innocent daughters. Dennis is bound to his wife by pity, as Scobie was to his; but, unlike Scobie, he is willing to cast off his responsibility to his wife in the hope that he will find happiness with Rose. Helen invites Mrs. Dennis to her home, and the unhappy wife asks her husband's mistress to pity her. In this tense and brilliant scene Greene brings all the issues in the drama into focus. Michael runs after his wife, for he cannot disallow the passionate pity that he feels for her. Bewildered, Rose turns to the priest, but the best he can say to her is, "You've got a lifetime to fool yourself in. It's a long time, to keep forgetting that poor hysterical woman who has a right to need him." [2] Overcome with pity and grief, Rose says:

You tell me if I go off with him he'll be unhappy for a lifetime. If I stay here, I'll have nothing but that closet and this—this living room. And you tell me there's hope and I can pray. Who to? Don't talk to me about God and the saints. I don't believe in your God who took away your legs and wants to take away Michael. I don't believe in your Church and your Holy Mother of God. I don't believe.   (59)

Rose can find no other solution for her grief but suicide; like Scobie in *The Heart of the Matter*, she dies uttering a prayer: "Our Father who art . . . who art . . . Bless Mother, Nanny and Sister Marie-Louise, and please God don't let school start again ever" (60). Rose reverts to the innocence of her childhood as she takes her life. But her death is not completely futile: Teresa defies Helen. No longer will Teresa fear death; symbolically she makes her bed in the living room, the room in which Rose has died; thus she denies Helen's fear of death and exhibits her faith in a forgiving God.

The Living Room ends on a note of perplexity, as it asks the audience if God is as simple as an equation, as clear as air? Will He damn for all eternity a creature whose dilemma seems insoluble by human standards? And this is in essence the problem of *The Heart of the Matter*. *The Living Room* deals with Roman Catholicism as a factor that emphasizes the individual's responsibility to himself and to a code. In Rose, the futility of life without love is described. The conception of her death may perhaps be better understood in the light of Scobie's suicide and of Sarah Miles's dedication to God in *The End of the Affair,* for Greene seems again in the play to question an orthodox Roman Catholic attitude towards suicide and salvation. But Rose's suicide need not be viewed in the same perspective with Scobie's death and Sarah Miles's physical decline. The play presents the issue clearly, dramatically, and economically, and the knowledge of Greene's preoccupation with this theme merely enhances.

Through Father Browne, as with Father Rank, Greene reasserts a favorite motif, the "appalling" nature of the mercy of God. Father Browne insists that no one knows what Rose was thinking at the precise moment of her death and that God can be no less forgiving than a woman—a line that comes almost verbatim from *The Heart of the Matter.* The fact that James cannot give Rose the help she needs at the moment she needs it contributes to the tragedy. In *The Heart of the Matter,* Father Rank is more convincing as a priest than as a character involved in precipitating the tragedy, while in the drama Father Browne contributes to the dilemma and hastens the tragedy. His words at the end of the play recover the general order of the Church. Again, as in Elizabethan drama, the person of greatest authority reasserts a general order before releasing the audience.

Perhaps the most interesting aspect of the play, aside from the dilemma, is Greene's use of the principal symbol of the living room, the room inhabited by the elderly sisters and the only one in a large house in which there has been no death. The room is, on a literal level, the expression of their fear of death; yet it is symbolic too of the narrowing of human experience into a restricted sphere which seems somehow, and perhaps paradoxically, to be Hope. This hope is a reaffirmation, and through Teresa Greene exploits the belief in the mercy of God and in a life after death. The eccentricity of the room, its furniture, the fact that it is on the third floor of an old house indicate the limited and thwarted perspective of the human being seeking a partial understanding of God's justice in the world. The living room is life; hence Rose's suicide in it derives greater meaning, and the "hint of an explanation," to use Greene's own term, offered by the dramatist is more readily appreciated.

The character who is best drawn and who demonstrates most ably Greene's ability in the sphere of the drama is Helen Browne, a "good" woman. The tragedy revolves upon her meddling; but whether this meddling is divinely inspired or not is a consideration that, although provocative, does not add to the tragic inevitability of the dilemma. Helen meddles. Her reasons are to her clear and cogent, but whether they are right or not is moot; it is sufficient to know that her reasons bring about the suicide. It is through Helen Browne, as well as through Rose Pemberton, that Greene advances the theme of the play: Which is the greater sin? To cut oneself off from grace, as Rose would do in living with Michael outside the "living room"? Or to sin and remain near the source of grace and the possibility of salvation?

To repeat, Helen Browne is a good woman, in the bosom of the Church. Yet she is scheming, calculating, cruel, and insensitive. She is a self-willed despot who insists on controlling the destiny of her niece, proclaiming her right to care for the girl's position as a Roman Catholic. In conception, Helen Browne is close to François Mauriac's Brigitte Pian of *La Pharisienne* who, as does Helen, insists on dominating the spirit of her husband and her stepchildren. Helen is a hypocrite, but she is not evil. Men may hate such people—but not God. The important point is that through Helen's meddling, others are made aware of the reality of God. Helen makes her influence felt upon her brother James and upon her sister Teresa; and as she succeeds in making Rose's suicide inevitable, she succeeds in keeping her within the Church. After Rose's death, when Helen attempts to keep Teresa from sleeping in the living room, she is, in a real sense, denying the teaching of her Church that the dead do not die. If the living room is symbolic of hope, then Helen denies hope. She judges and arranges life, for she fears death. "Stop it," says her brother James. "We've had enough of this foolishness. God isn't unmerciful the way a woman can be. You've been afraid too long. It's time for you to rest, my darling, It's time for you to rest" (67).

The Living Room ends on the same note as *The Heart of the Matter*. The priest remains to reestablish, as best he can, the norm of the Church; he insists that the living are not forced to believe, as Helen does, that Rose is damned. He insists that, although Rose had spit at the word "prayer" and had hated God in the minutes before she died, He alone can judge her motives, for hate and love are often one. And Teresa affirms this statement when she turns to Helen and says, "Why shouldn't I sleep here? We're not afraid of the child. And there'd be no better room for me to fall asleep in forever than the room where Rose died" (67).

II   The Potting Shed

The Potting Shed makes use of the Lazarus theme, one which Greene had earlier employed in a short story called "The Second Death." The story, dated 1929 in *Nineteen Stories*, describes the life of a man who had once been given up for dead. "Suppose I had been dead," he says to a friend who, one learns later, had himself profited from a miracle. "I believed it then, you know, and so did my mother. . . . I went straight for a couple of years. I thought it might be a sort of second chance. Then things got fogged and somehow. . . ." [3] As the dying man prepares for his second death, he begs his friend to reassure him that the first death had been nothing but a dream. "It would be so dreadful . . . if it had been true, and I'd got to go through all that again. You don't know what things were going to happen to me in that dream. And they'd be worse now. . . . When one's dead there's no unconsciousness any more forever." [4] One will remember too that Greene's novel *The End of the Affair* employs a miracle as part of the thematic material.

The Potting Shed also makes use of the detective story framework that Greene utilizes in many of his entertainments and novels, and this dimension adds to the suspense and action of the play. As the play opens, the audience is confronted by a mystery. The Callifers are gathered at "Wild Grove" for the impending demise of old Callifer, the head of the family, who in his youth and vigorous middle age had preached an extreme rationalist belief. The mystery develops through Anne the granddaughter, who assumes a symbolic position in the drama akin to that of Ida Arnold in *Brighton Rock*, since it is she who precipitates the denouement. Neither James, old Callifer's younger son, nor his Uncle William Callifer has been summoned to "Wild Grove," once a great country seat but now an old house encroached upon by the chimneys and the mill towers of an industrial neighborhood.

Anne, however, sent James a telegram, and he has come to his father's deathbed hoping to learn what in his life makes him incapable of experiencing any deep-felt, human emotion. "Sara, what's wrong with me?" he asks his divorced wife. "You're not alive," she says. "Sometimes I wanted to make you angry or sorry, to hurt you. But you never felt pain." [5] His inability to participate in the human environment gives James the only pain that he understands, and this pain is more an absence of feeling than anything else. He has no memory beyond waking up in a sick bed in his fourteenth year and wondering what accident or circumstance had turned his parents against him. The mystery is somehow connected with the potting shed at the bottom of the garden, amongst the laurels; and James fears the place.

In the second act it is discovered that, at the age of fourteen, the boy had hanged himself in the shed. He had fallen under the influence of Uncle William, a Roman Catholic convert who had become a priest. The boy's father had rudely disillusioned his beliefs in the "mysteries" of the Church; as a result of his father's rational "awakening," James had attempted suicide. The body had been discovered by the gardener, Potter, who, on trying to revive the boy, had assured himself that he was dead. William had come into the potting shed and promised God his only valuable possession—his faith—to spare the boy he loved. And God had struck the bargain.

James, who had come back to life with no memory of his innocence or of his love, is a living dead man. Fearing the revelation of the "miracle" and what it would do to the reputation of the rationalist Callifer, his parents had withdrawn from James. To affirm the miracle would be to affirm the existence of God. Mrs. Callifer says, "Oh, the Callifers knew everything. It was all right to doubt the existence of God as your grandfather did in the time of Darwin. Doubt—that was human liberty. But my generation, we didn't doubt, we knew" (73). And Mrs. Callifer says of her husband, "All his life he'd written on the necessity of proof. Proof. And then a proof was pushed under his nose, at the bottom of his own garden, in the potting shed. . . . I could hear him saying to himself, 'Must I recall all those books and start again?'" (64-65).

James's meeting with his uncle in Nottingham affords him the knowledge he needs to understand himself, and it provides him with the information about his past that allows him to exist in the present and for the future. When he tells his wife that he can now love her because he acknowledges God, she is as frightened by his belief as before she had been frightened by his lack of conviction or, as she phrases it, his love of Nothing. What convinces James of the reality of God is his understanding of Uncle William's life without faith, once God had heard his prayer. A room without faith, his uncle's presbytery in Nottingham—in some ways reminiscent of the "living" room of the earlier play—is, James says, like a marriage without love. God is in the world and to deny God is to deny life: "Something happened to me, that's all, like a street accident. I don't want God. But He's there—it's no good pretending. He's in my lungs like air" (71). The play ends on a symbolic note of optimism. Discovered asleep on the window seat, Anne tells of her dream—she had found a lion asleep in the potting shed; on awakening, it had licked her hand.

The Potting Shed is a better play than its predecessor, for it deals more economically and more dramatically with human motives—especially with fear—despite the fact that at times the action is static. The added dimension of mystery, introduced through the innocent character Anne, contributes to the effectiveness of the revelation of the suicide. As does Ida Arnold in *Brighton Rock,* Anne emphasizes the necessity of admitting the truth, of bringing into the light the actions of the past so that they may lend meaning to the present and to the future. In this sense she is humanity, bright and alert. And the potting shed that James and his parents have feared for so long is, as was the living room, the place of hope, the place of life; it is not to be feared and shunned, but to be acknowledged and accepted. Once its importance in the life of the Callifers has been admitted, it becomes a tool shed for gardening equipment. Those who had feared it had feared the truth of the miracle that took place within it thirty years before the action of the play.

What lends the play its atmosphere and contributes to its effectiveness is Greene's handling of the Lazarus theme. In allowing James to admit his death and accept his return to life as a miracle—the result of his uncle's bargain with God—Greene manages to establish clearly the major symbolism of the drama. Only upon the death of H. C. Callifer, who hypocritically guarded the rationalist values upon which the family prestige depended, can the truth be revealed. The number thirty is, of course, used to suggest the Christian idea of betrayal, and James's role as scapegoat becomes more readily understandable. There are other symbols used in the play, some of which are perhaps again derived from T. S. Eliot. The polluted river, the encroaching industrial city, the harmony of the garden, the baying dog, the hanged man all have their echoes in *The Waste Land* and in "Ash Wednesday." But these symbols are so integrated into the fabric of the play that an understanding of the theme does not depend on their explication.

The Potting Shed was written with two third acts, one for the American production in 1957 and another for the British production of 1958. There are minor textual changes in the first two acts that add little if anything to the general development of the play's action. But the American version lists the time of the play as autumn, and the final scene takes place during the Christmas season, thus allowing Greene to capitalize on the Christian symbolism of the Nativity. The British version sets the play in the spring, and the implication is that the action culminates around Easter, although nothing is specifically mentioned. This setting in time, it seems, is surer symbolism; for the idea of rebirth is the one that sustains the activity of the drama. The potting shed and the garden become more meaningful.

The third act in the American production has James explain his new-found faith to his wife Sara, capitalizing on the broken-marriage theme. In the American version Sara is softer, more willing to understand her husband's new belief. The British version, however, has James explain his new-found belief to his mother who is, after all, of greater importance in the overall meaning of the play, for she has for thirty years protected her husband from the implications of the miracle. In the British production Sara is less agreeable about accepting James's new faith. She had been frightened by his belief in Nothing, and she is now equally alarmed by his belief in God. Whether he will succeed in remarrying her is left tentative. But both third acts end with the optimistic telling of Anne's dream of the lion licking her hand.

The miracle in *The Potting Shed* is strongly reminiscent of the miracle in *The End of the Affair*. Sarah Miles asks God to spare Bendrix' life, offering to stop seeing him. After God answers her prayer, she proceeds to greater and greater awareness of His existence. Unlike Sarah, William Callifer goes on in his existence without faith until he is given the proof of the miracle. Again the question of grace is left in abeyance, adding a provocative titillation for the reader who is more interested in religious controversy than in drama.

III   The Complaisant Lover

"It's unfair," says Victor Rhodes, the cuckolded husband to Mary, his wife, ". . . that we're only dressed for a domestic comedy." [6] Earlier in *The Complaisant Lover,* he says, before the knowledge of his wife's unfaithfulness is known to him, "I can assure you there are very few situations in life that a joke won't ease" (2). And there are many jokes in the play and many puns. Although *The Complaisant Lover* adds enormously to Greene's stature as a playwright and to his popularity as an entertainer, it is by no means the provocative study that his earlier plays had been. *The Complaisant Lover,* furthermore, makes no specific reference to religious matters; the only commentary made on the moral appropriateness of the chief actors' complaisance is oblique at best. But certain ambiguities of speech and humor may be construed to suggest a subterranean religious feeling.

In the characterization of Mary, Greene draws against a background of literary "emancipated" women. There are echoes of Ibsen's Nora and of Shaw's Candida, but the play is uniquely "Greenien" in the mixture of sadness and sweetness that is used to describe the predicament of the lover who seeks in his escapades a knowledge of experience, not of innocence. Clive Root has always loved married women; and, when Anne Howard offers him her innocent love on whatever terms he desires, he is forced to refuse her, for as he says: " '. . . Perhaps I fall in love with experience. . . . Perhaps I don't care for innocence. . . . Perhaps it's envy of other men, and I want to prove myself better than they are' " (12). There is interesting counterpoint developed in Anne's infatuation for Clive, for Mary's adolescent son is smitten with Anne, giving her such tokens of esteem as a badly stuffed mouse and an electric eye that doesn't work. This is clever handling and a further illustration of Greene's growth as a playwright, for it suggests a fragile irony that would have escaped him in the earlier, heavier works.

The climax of the play develops in a hotel room in Amsterdam where Mary and Clive have gone for a holiday, Mary having invented a friend called Jane Crane to put her husband Victor off the scent. Victor arrives a day before he is expected; he finds Mary in her hotel room, the mythical Jane gone, and Clive close by. He suspects nothing, but Clive, to precipitate the action, pays a bellboy 100 guilders to pen a poisonous note informing the husband of his wife's infidelity. When the note arrives in London, Victor, annoyed at his failure to understand the situation, confronts Mary with the facts. She begs him not to force her to a decision, for the habit of marriage is sixteen years strong in her. Like Henry and Sarah Miles in *The End of the Affair*, they have grown used to one another's company, and the habits of domestic life are too strong to be easily severed. But Clive Root is not Maurice Bendrix, nor could he be in the comic context of the play. Root's jealousy and his mania for possession are equally as strong as Bendrix'; but he has his knowledge of past love affairs to sustain him. He realizes that he will accept Rhodes's terms and remain Mary's lover, until one day he will find it no longer possible to be complaisant. And then the end of the affair.

The moral commentary is, of course, obliquely made in the final moments of the play. The long years of married habit, of domestic comfort, and of children's teeth and shoes and holidays will indeed intrude upon and disillusion the lovers. In the final analysis, the husband and wife relationship will prove vital, and the family will be preserved. The domestic comedy will have run its course, and the routine blessings of home comfort and everyday morality will be reasserted.

The Complaisant Lover is a far cry from the earlier plays that dealt heavily with a religious theme. This play represents Greene asserting his command over a comic form, just as he did in *Our Man in Havana*. That once again he chooses a cliché situation and then invests it with a charm and grace peculiarly his own offers still further testimony of his consummate artistry. And the cuckolded husband—asserting his prerogative as husband, understanding his wife's yearning for romance and her need to be protected—emerges as one of Greene's strongest and most sensible heroes, despite his penchant for grotesque tricks and schoolboy humor. The amoral rationale of the play is sustained by the charm and wit of the lines and by Greene's remarkable sense of the ridiculous—early apparent in several of the short stories, but most clearly evident in *Our Man in Havana*. The introduction of Doctor Van Droog in the Amsterdam hotel room is little more than farcical invention; but, in the general handling of the climactic scene, it is sheer brilliance, punctuating as it does the ridiculousness of the situation and accentuating at the same time the moral obliquity that on the surface characterizes the play.

The fact that Victor is a dentist is significant too. One remembers Dr. Tench of *The Power and the Glory,* and Greene's reference to the carious mouth, the symbol that he borrowed from Eliot's *The Waste Land.* The carious mouth is gone; for it does not belong in a domestic comedy. But the reference to teeth, the fact that the lover has a badly filled tooth, adds to the sense of the ridiculous and the absurd. All in all, *The Complaisant Lover* is brilliant invention and Graham Greene at his entertaining best. And like every other piece that he has done, it emphasizes his ability to adapt to new conditions, to new media.

As a writer of detective stories, novels, entertainments, movie scripts, and stage plays, Graham Greene has managed to create one of the most significant bodies of literature in the twentieth century. His first two plays are first-rate drama. They are not "religious" plays, although they do attest the existence of God and make capital use of a religious theme. They are primarily strong and realistic portrayals of human beings caught in emotional difficulties. *The Complaisant Lover* may be better theater than its predecessors, but it is not as good drama. Greene is better, in the final analysis, when he deals with human beings caught up in a tragic human condition of their own devising than when he treats a farcically contrived plot, no matter how funny.

CHAPTER 7

The Catholic as Novelist Once More

FRANÇOIS MAURIAC'S problem as a writer who happens to be a Catholic has been similar to and yet unlike Greene's. In 1936 Mauriac wrote an account of the development of his religious convictions to refute the charge leveled at him by André Gide that he sought permission to be a Catholic without having to burn his books:

> If I refuse to accept this reproach of Gide's it is not because I think I am innocent. I am probably more guilty than a man who is tugged both ways, who wants to write his books without missing heaven and to win heaven without foregoing his books. It is putting it too mildly to say that I "do not lose sight of Mammon." The fact is that I am in the front line of his besiegers. But the impossibility of serving two masters does not necessarily mean the forsaking of one for the other to the extent of losing sight of the forsaken One or losing awareness of His presence and power. And even if this sight and awareness were lost, we would still be wearing the untearable livery of the Master we had betrayed; we would still, by force or free will, belong to His house.[1]

And he then says: "Above all I liked to be persuaded by Pascal that a search was always possible, that there could always be a voyage of discovery within revealed truth" (19). Mauriac tells his reader that early in life he became aware that, born a Catholic, he could never live outside the boundaries of his religion. This knowledge led him to criticize his religion inadvertently, and many readers detected an ambiguity of point of view in his early works. Nevertheless, he continued to write within the borders of Catholicism and became the object of mistrust and contempt to many of his fellow-Catholics: "I knew that the Christian God demanded everything. I knew that he had no part in the flesh and that the world of nature and the world of grace were two and inimical. Pascal taught me this with an almost excessive ruthlessness, and I knew it to be terrifyingly true" (20).

The Catholic critics, therefore, were not as Mauriac tells his reader, unjust in detecting and censuring the tendency toward Jansenism and Manichaeism that is to be found in such novels as *Flesh and Blood* and *Thérèse Desqueyroux;* he admits that he too could discern the element of corruption prowling over his work "in the way it prowls over cemeteries which are nevertheless dominated by the Cross." And he goes on to say: "I always put myself on guard against the aesthetic side of present-day Catholicism, and its emotional appeal, however sublime, at once excites my mistrust. I long with all my soul for the 'consolations of religion,' but I know at what price they must be bought. I know all about peace in suffering, and I know that bitterness with which past sins penetrate through present grace" (25).

Both Greene and Mauriac then are aware of the difficulties involved in writing against a Roman Catholic background, and both writers are also aware of the fact that, to render the highest justice to God, the force of evil must be appreciated—even if, at times, appreciating the beauty of evil seems a questioning of the orthodox preachings of their Church. Both Greene and Mauriac are concerned not only with observing life but with creating the experience of it. They bring living people into world—complex, inscrutable, and made unhappy by their lack of identity with the source of good. Both Greene and Mauriac, in a very real sense, lose their identity in the subjects of their creation; hence the charge that they "connive" with the devil. Mauriac says: "If there is a reason for the existence of the novelist on earth it is this: to show the element which holds out against God in the highest and noblest characters—the innermost evils and dissimulations; and also to light up the secret source of sanctity in creatures who seem to us to have failed" (59). To say that in their works they stress Roman Catholic theology at the expense of psychological or artistic truth is to misunderstand completely the nature and function of their art.

Speaking of *The Power and the Glory,* Mauriac says of Graham Greene in *Great Men:* "The work of an English Catholic novelist—of an Englishman returning to Catholicism—such as Graham Greene's *The Power and the Glory,* at first always gives me the sensation of being in a foreign land. To be sure, I find there my spiritual fatherland, and it is into the heart of a familiar mystery that Graham Greene introduces me. But everything takes place as though I were making my way into an old estate through a concealed door. . . ." [2]

Mauriac goes on to point out that the French Catholic enters the edifice of his religion by the front door; that, as a schoolboy, he is versed in the various schisms and heresies that comprise the official history of his Church. The convert to Roman Catholicism, on the other hand, enters the edifice of his religion through the archway of his early upbringing and religious training. The religious influences felt as a child and a catechism so like and yet so unlike the Roman Catholic's consciously interfere and intrude when the man makes his choice later on. Mauriac may envy Maritain and other converts to Catholicism for the freedom of their choice, as he tells the reader in the second chapter of *God and Mammon;* but he is, nevertheless, confused when reading Greene. Greene's world seems alien to him, although its mysteries are clear. The explanation of this strangeness is perhaps not too difficult.

The melodrama, the key to much of Greene's work, perhaps that very aspect that makes Mauriac feel an alien, was set by early reading in the romantic stories of Marjorie Bowen and Rider Haggard; but Charles Dickens, Joseph Conrad, Henry James, and Ford Madox Ford taught him how to handle his themes and to develop his plots. His early apprenticeship as movie critic for the *Spectator* sharpened his perceptions of the nature of melodrama and what could be achieved through it. The political activities of the 1930's perhaps indicated to him that melodrama was the best means of echoing the times. In *Journey Without Maps,* he wrote:

To-day our world seems peculiarly susceptible to brutality. There is a touch of nostalgia in the pleasure we take in gangster novels, in characters who have so agreeably simplified their emotions that they have begun living again at a level below the cerebral. We, like Wordsworth, are living after a war and a revolution, and these half-castes fighting with bombs between the cliffs of skyscrapers seem more likely than we to be aware of Proteus rising from the sea. It is not, of course, that one wishes to stay forever at that level, but when one sees to what unhappiness, to what peril of extinction centuries of cerebration have brought us, one sometimes has a curiosity to discover if one can from what we have come, to recall at which point we went astray.[3]

Greene's conversion to Roman Catholicism seems a logical step in his intellectual development. In the teaching of the Roman Church, he found a hint of an explanation, to use his own term, for many of the problems that vexed him as a child and as a man, and a partial explanation for suffering and misery; hence come the questioning and the probing that so many readers remark in such mature works as *The Heart of the Matter* and *The End of the Affair*. The mixture of melodrama and religious background first appeared in Greene's works in *Brighton Rock*, but his attitudes were discernible in earlier books.

Ultimately Greene differs from Mauriac in method rather than in theme, for Greene writes his novels and entertainments within the traditional forms of the English novel. Greene's reading of Dickens' novels accounts for many of his seedy characters and for his grotesque children, his Else and young Parkis; it also accounts in part for the social commentary and for the mixture of sentimentality and social ire of such works as *England Made Me*, *It's a Battlefield*, and *Brighton Rock*. Greene's reading of Conrad taught him the nature of allegory—as did his reading of Bunyan—and the importance of ethical choice. Lord Jim stands behind the whiskey priest, just as Axel Heyst, who cultivates pity as a form of contempt, stands behind Arthur Rowe and Major Scobie; and Marlow and Heyst stand behind Fowler and Querry. Moreover, Conrad's anti-heroes relate in the same way to Pinkie Brown and James Raven. It is not surprising, therefore, that Greene says of Conrad in his book *In Search of a Character:* "Reading Conrad—the volume called *Youth* for the sake of *Heart of Darkness*—the first time since I abandoned him about 1932 because his influence on me was too great and too disastrous. The heavy hypnotic style falls around me again, and I am aware of the poverty of my own. Perhaps now I have lived long enough with my poverty to be safe from corruption. One day I will again read *Victory*. And *The Nigger*."[4]

Greene's reading in Henry James taught him concern for style, for correctness, for the dissection of human motive; James also taught him how to manipulate the stuff of evil while unfolding the complexities of character:

There was no victory for human beings, that was his conclusion; you were punished in your way, whether you were of God's or the Devil's party. James believed in the supernatural, but he saw evil as an equal force with good. Humanity was cannon fodder in a war too balanced ever to be concluded. If he had been guilty of the supreme egotism of preserving his own existence, he left the material, in his profound unsparing analysis, for rendering even egotism the highest kind of justice, of giving the devil his due.[5]

As cited before, with the death of James, Greene wrote in his essay on François Mauriac, the English novel lost "the religious sense," and with it "the importance of the human act." [6]

Furthermore Greene, unlike Mauriac, is in the unenviable position of writing his books for a predominantly Protestant audience —one which still nourishes a distrust of Catholicism that goes back to the English Reformation. If at times Greene seems belligerent and insistent about the Roman Catholicism of his characters, it is perhaps because he is aware of, remembering his origins, the hostility of his readers. And the fact that so many Protestant readers have seen fit to question Greene's personal orthodoxy is in itself an indication that he has achieved some measure of success in fabricating controversial stories of violence and suspense within a framework of Roman Catholic belief, a belief that suggests treachery to the spiritual fitness of many Protestants. But it also seems so to many Catholics as well.

François Mauriac, on the other hand, writes to a predominantly Catholic audience—to one aware of the implications of Jansenism, the religious controversy between Bossuet and Fenelon, and the hundreds of years of Church influence on the hearts and intellects of Frenchmen. Mauriac has written eloquently in *Great Men* of the influence of Pascal, Voltaire, Rousseau, Maurice de Guérin, and others on his works. Both Elsie Pell and Gerald Moloney have recently commented on the literary sources of Mauriac's work. But in *God and Mammon* he says revealingly: "I can say with truth that no book has moved me more deeply than a simple and innocent novel called *Feet of Clay* which I adored when I was fourteen. It was the work of an old and virtuous woman called Zenaide de Fleuriot, and it was full of imagination and sensibility." [7] Imagination and sensibility are keynotes of the Mauriac novels, just as melodrama and suspense are keynotes of the Greene novels. Like Greene—whose indebtedness to

Charlotte M. Yonge's *The Little Duke,* a work of innocence, is testified to by *The Ministry of Fear*—Mauriac's youthful sensibilities were moved by the exploits of innocence abroad in a black and white universe, the innocent taking the form of a freckle-faced girl with the lovely name of Armelle Trahec. Yet Mauriac admits in the same passage that, when asked to name the writers who have most influenced him, he replies automatically "Balzac and Dostoyevsky."

This is to say that a youthful imagination, stimulated by the innocent exploits of Mlle. Trahec, was disciplined by a rigorous training in the classics of the French novel and in the psychological analyses of the pre-Freudian analyst, Dostoevski—an influence that can also be ascribed to Greene. In *Great Men* Mauriac tells his reader that he also read avidly the writings of the iconoclastic Anatole France; that, despite Flaubert's anti-Catholicism, that writer's skill and understanding impressed him deeply, particularly Flaubert's liking for those who threw themselves into emotional extremes, perhaps as do Thérèse Desqueyroux and Maria Cross, as do Jean Pélouèyre and old Villenave. Stendhal stands behind the partly romantic, partly realistic love scenes of *La Pharisienne,* as he does in those many many scenes in which the psychology of the characters seems to shape itself on the very page. And Balzac and Zola stand behind those many novels which are centered on the Bordeaux countryside—novels in which the traditions of French family life, its greed and hypocrisy, its humor and dignity, are carefully and poignantly developed.

Mauriac is not a realist, however, in the sense that Zola is a realist; rather, he is a realist in a moral sense. As in the works of Balzac, the writer who automatically springs to his lips when his literary influences are called into question, Mauriac's works move quietly, the observations keenly made and the scenes fully realized, the religious and moral implications rising insistently above action that might at times verge on the sensational. Even the sensational aspects of the Desqueyroux murder trial seem folded into the fabric of the novel in *Thérèse Desqueyroux,* for there the emphasis falls on the instinctive evil of the heroine whose face reveals the pitilessness of her character only in moments of lethargy; a heroine in whom, nevertheless, her author finds the germs of spirituality, and through whom the power of grace may be felt.

[144]

The traditions of the French novel ultimately define the method that Mauriac follows in portraying themes that are animated by a Roman Catholic understanding of the effects of sin on the soul and of the all-pervasive power of grace. No wonder he feels an alien when he first reads Greene. The mystery may be the same, but the approach to the mystery has been determined by the conventions of the English novel and Greene's English literary heritage. The similarities that exist in the works of these two writers, startling enough at first, become curious contrasts in the final analysis.

There is one more point, however, that needs to be made. It would be foolish to say that Greene has not read Mauriac's novels and Mauriac, Greene's. And it is interesting to observe the reciprocal influences that can be seen in their works. It would seem that Greene has borrowed more from Mauriac than Mauriac from Greene. Greene's drama *The Living Room*, for example, shows a remarkable similarity of theme and character to Mauriac's *La Pharisienne*. Greene's drama concerns the efforts of Helen Browne, the elderly and misguided Catholic, to keep her niece Rose from abandoning her religion by becoming the common wife of a married man. *La Pharisienne* recounts the exertions of a stepmother, Brigitte Pian, to impose the precepts of Roman Catholic dogma on her wards. Mauriac describes with brilliant insight and a penetrating awareness of religious considerations Brigitte's gradual recognition of herself. The lady of the Pharisees gradually sees her image; but she is not appalled. She slowly becomes aware of her hypocrisy, but she feels that she is not evil. And this is much the situation that Mauriac develops in *The Desert of Love*, and that Greene himself has come extremely close to in *The End of the Affair*. For the heroine of *The Desert of Love*, Maria Cross, is much like Sarah Miles. Maria is promiscuous, but she is also tender, human, loving. After an accident she recognizes her hypocrisy and gives up an attempt to seduce her physician's son, the impressionable Raymond Courrèges. Maria finds at the end of her youth an ambiguous awareness of the love of God in her relationship with Bertrand de Larouselle, her husband's son by another wife. She succeeds in convincing herself that her love for Bertrand is a love of the god he loves. And perhaps it is. The important fact is that her hypocrisy, if it is hypocrisy, makes others aware of the reality of God. One knows who Brigitte Pian and Maria Cross are, and is better for recognizing the grain of holiness that is covered by the crust of hypocrisy. Mauriac's triumph is that he makes these people come alive. And Greene's Helen Browne is just such a character as Brigitte Pian.

These characters are studies in misguided and, to some extent, unintentional hypocrisy (as is Lady Marchmain in Waugh's *Brideshead Revisited*); and they indicate the concern that both Greene and Mauriac have with similar themes. Further similarities could be drawn, but they would prove little more than that Greene has read Mauriac and Mauriac, Greene; that both are dealing with expressions of life within a Roman Catholic framework; and that both are different because they have different backgrounds.

Both writers, dealing with individuals in their relationship to God, and, consequently, to their fellow men, develop their themes according to their own geniuses. And in this realm all comparisons prove fruitless. The point is that within the confines of the novel the work of both Catholics is determined by their origins, their cultural traditions, and the times.

CHAPTER 8

Literary Opinions

A T least six books, listed in the Selected Bibliography, and several scores of scholarly articles have been written about Greene; and in many of these the terms "Manichaeist," "Augustinist," "Quietist," "Pelagianist," "Jansenist," and "Existentialist" have been used to describe the philosophical or theological bent that Greene "pursues." These terms, perhaps, need clarification, and I should like here to refer to significant Greene scholarship while commenting on the explanations.

In *Esquisses anglaises*[1] Claire Eliane Engel discusses the possibility that the Greene *oeuvre* is tinged with Jansenism. Engel states that it has been possible to discern in Greene's novels both fatality and predestination, and that many have put the theme of flight and pursuit down to this Calvinist orientation. In other words, the man who throws himself into sin is dedicated to evil, and death is the wages of sin. Only God can liberate the sinner by His grace.

The Calvinistic ethic, then, may be interpreted as the *raison d'être* for the chase motif found in a good many Greene novels. However, this argument fails to consider sufficiently that the chase motif is a standard device of the detective story; indeed, that it is a traditional motif in literature of many cultures, and that Greene, especially in such a work as *Brighton Rock*, remains within the conventions of the type of novel he writes. Accepting Jansenism as a ruling philosophy would lead to the conclusion that the plight of the Greene hero is not of his making, that it is predetermined, and that a particular sinner is doomed to hell or to be expedited to heaven according to the destiny God has ordained for him. Engel admits, however, that Greene's religion is not "une question de formalisme," that his ideas, whether or not they tend to Jansenism, are not rigid.

Evelyn Waugh in his review of *The Heart of the Matter* cited earlier finds the philosophical climate that pervades the Greene world to be one of Quietism. Quietism is defined as a tendency to religious devotion rather than a definite theological belief. It stresses Christian perfection as a state of uninterrupted contemplation of God, and it insists that the soul remains passive under a divine influence. Contemplation, quiet and serene, does not necessarily depend on the tenets of orthodox belief; rather, it succeeds by eliminating the thought of punishment or reward in another life. The Quietist makes faith the paramount consideration, and he insists that contemplation of God makes the necessity of works negligible to produce a condition for salvation.

Waugh says of Major Scobie: "We are told that he is actuated throughout by the love of God. A love, it is true, that falls short of trust, but a love, we must suppose, which sanctifies his sins. That is the heart of the matter. Is such a sacrifice feasible? . . ." [2] Such an attitude, Waugh insists, would mean that one has to be as wicked as Pinkie Brown before he runs into the danger of being damned. This estimate of Greene's "devotional" tendencies in his novels would, if carried further, deprive the novels of dramatic conflict, of psychological motivation.

Walter Allen, in an interesting essay about Greene, first published in *Penguin New Writing*,[3] discusses the theology that informs Greene's novels in terms of Augustinism and Pelagianism. Augustinism accepts something of the Manichaean heresy which insists on a duality of nature. The Manichaean believes that all matter is evil and that man therefore is essentially evil. (Man is, however, sometimes rescued by an arbitrary selection on the part of God.) St. Augustine adds to this the idea of the fortunate fall: there is evil in the world, but it is put there so that man can rise above it; and, by rising above it, he proves his kinship to God. Greene himself in the epigraph to *The Lawless Roads* quotes from Cardinal Newman, and in the quotation the basis of the Christian aspects of Augustinism is apparent: "I can only answer, that either there is no Creator, or this living society of men is in a true sense discarded from His presence . . . *if* there be a God, *since* there is a God, the human race is implicated in some terrible aboriginal calamity." Nineteenth-century echoes are also heard herein.

In a world with no hope and in one without God, Allen goes

on, all that man sees about him impresses him with a sense of the profound mystery which is beyond human solution. For the average person, Augustinism in its human aspects will appear nasty, seedy, unlikable, brutish, often cruel, often despicable. This philosophy then, in great part, accounts for Greene's people, his Acky and his Prewitt, his Minty and his Farrant.

Pelagianism, on the other hand, insists that man is naturally good, "but is perverted by external factors, by society as such if he is an anarchist, by the capitalist system if he is a Marxist, or by the family" (149). The Pelagian would go so far as to deny the reality of evil, for his emphasis would be placed on man as one who has within himself the power to control his destiny.

Allen maintains that Greene has adopted in his works the Augustinian concept of evil and that this affords him a basis for evaluating the ills of the world. He adds that Augustinism offers the same possibilities for heroism in the twentieth century that its non-Christian counterpart offered for the sixteenth and early seventeenth centuries:

In the understanding and assessment of the human situation in such an age of violence as our own the Augustinian, for whom evil is endemic in man's nature, is at a tremendous advantage. How tremendous may be seen if we compare the present age with an age of similar violence, the Elizabethan period and the first half of the seventeenth century. England had its burnings and its martyrdoms, its civil wars, yet in comparison with continental Europe was relatively peaceful. But how the Englishman reacted to those years of violence may be seen in the plays of the great Elizabethans: Marlowe, Shakespeare, Jonson, Webster, Tourneur, Ford, are horrified but fascinated; yet they can assimilate violence, the evil; it is part and parcel of their emotional world; it is what happens to man when the order, the natural and the supernatural, that curbs him, is broken. It does not surprise them, because the jungle is, as it were, man's natural state. (150)

This appraisal of Allen's seems to me most logical, for it allows the possibility of heroism. The Greene universe is not limited to the evil that Manichaeism advocates as the prevailing aspect of life, nor to the predetermined world of Jansenist thought. By allowing for the possibility that man may rise above the evil that is endemic to his nature, Greene's hero may find heaven at the end of his journey. If not heaven, then in dying he may find heroism—

perhaps not the magnificent and bragging heroism of the world of Tamerlane, but at least the pitiful heroism of the Duchess of Malfi.

Not all of Greene's critics, however, are disposed to label him primarily a religious writer. George Woodcock[4] and Arthur Calder-Marshall [5] maintain that Greene's principal concern is not with religion but with the relationship of man to society, "with the individual as victim, and society the villain." Their claim is that Greene is a good man fallen among Catholics.

Kenneth Allott and Miriam Farris,[6] in one of the most comprehensive books of Greene criticism to appear, admit the strong religious tone that pervades the novels; but they indicate that this preoccupation is merely a facet of the Greene universe. They stress the idea that Greene's preoccupation with good and evil made itself apparent in his early youth, long before he adopted Roman Catholicism. They insist on the idea of the corrupted childhood leading to a predilection for horror and violence in later life, and they define the Greene canon in terms of "obsessions."

The obsessions that Allott and Farris discuss in their critique are, first, those depending on the divided mind—the world of *The Man Within;* second, those dealing with the fallen world— *Stamboul Train* and *It's a Battlefield;* third, those in which the theme of pity is exploited—*The Ministry of Fear, The Power and the Glory,* and *The Heart of the Matter.* The central obsession, that which lends unity to the others, is to Allott and Farris the terror of life and its origins in the early years; it is the corruption of the state of innocence that is the dominating motif in the work of Greene. Fear of life accounts for the theme of damnation; and this theme finds particular expression in the sin of the whiskey priest of *The Power and the Glory* and in Scobie's suicide in *The Heart of the Matter.*

Since Allott and Farris prefer to deal with Greene's "obsessions," they fail to reckon, with the power of the religious theme as a strong structural aspect of the novels. Certainly the preoccupations which they define in Greene's work are evident in the novels, but the religious element cannot be dismissed quite so easily. The theme of childhood betrayal which Greene so brilliantly develops in "The Basement Room" seems to be a secondary rather than a principal consideration in the mature novels.

In a very interesting and provocative study, *Graham Greene: témoin des temps tragiques*,[7] Paul Rostenne discusses the novels in terms of Sartrian Existentialism, an aspect of Greene scholarship that was developed in Chapter 5. According to Sartre, Existentialism insists on the cult of the individual, what he labels "le culte du moi." Sartrian Existentialism denies God and makes atheism the ruling philosophy. In his novels Sartre has caught the conflict of a hero versus a society that does not foster heroism. There is little reason, it seems, for judging the Greene hero as the exponent of such a philosophy, although there are certain superficial resemblances, particularly in Scobie and Fowler. The Greene hero chooses, despite his egotism, not so much "le culte du moi" as "le culte des autres"; for when Major Scobie commits suicide he does not deny the existence of God and glorify the idea of self; paradoxical as it may seem to the Existentialist, he affirms his relationship to God.

Gaétan Bernoville in an introductory essay to a study of the Catholicism of François Mauriac indicates strongly his disapproval of those who would label Greene primarily a theologian or even one whose preoccupations in his novels are exclusively religious. Bernoville indicates that in recent fiction a religious preoccupation has replaced the psychoanalytic preoccupation that dominated much of the literature of the 1920's and the 1930's. Bernoville considers Greene, as Greene considers himself, to be primarily and essentially a novelist; the Catholicism involved in the books is merely a device used to render his fable "captivating." [8]

One of the most sensible books of Greene criticism is *Graham Greene*, by Jacques Madaule, which discounts the influence of Claudel, Mauriac, and Bernanos; Madaule insists that Greene's chief problem as a writer who uses Catholicism as a theme in his work is the predominantly Protestant audience for which he writes; and he sees Greene's use of religion as flexible:

Le christianisme de Graham Greene est un christianisme réaliste, ce qui ne signifie pas du tout qu'il soit superstitieux. Greene a horreur de l'idéalisme et de l'optimisme que le protestantisme a paradoxalement développé dans le monde anglo-saxon. Cela produit, au bout du compte, des Ida Arnold et, dans un registre infiniment plus sympathique, des êtres tels que Miss Lehr et de son frère, qui recoivent très charitablement le prêtre fugitif, mais qui ne comprennent rien a ses "momeries." [9]

More recently John Atkins[10] and Francis Kunkel [11] have written books on Greene. Atkins's *Graham Greene* purports to be a biographical criticism, but is little more than a chronological listing of Greene's works and the events of his life. Kunkel's book is better. In *The Labyrinthine Ways of Graham Greene*, he explains Greene's use of religious subject matter, traces characters and themes, and analyzes situations. Kunkel considers recurrent patterns, situations, and symbols, and he evaluates literary and religious influences on Greene as a maturing artist.

But to return to Greene—he finds the theological harangues over his works difficult to understand. *Time*[12] quotes him: " 'I wrote a novel about a man who goes to hell—*Brighton Rock*— another about a man who goes to heaven—*The Power and the Glory*. Now I've simply written one about a man who goes to purgatory [*The Heart of the Matter*]. I don't know what all the fuss is about.' " One might add that *The End of the Affair* is a novel about a woman who goes to heaven, and *A Burnt-Out Case* is a novel about a man whose destination is debatable.

Notes and References

Unless otherwise specified the references to Greene's novels are to the Uniform Edition, published by William Heinemann, Ltd. The dates of original publication are included in the text and in the bibliography.

Preface

1. Thomas Merton, *The Seven Storey Mountain* (New York, 1948), p. 128.

2. Bertrand Russell, *The Impact of Science on Society* (New York, 1953), pp. 91-92.

Chapter One

1. *The Prelude*, Book VI, 11. 621-40.

2. "Locksley Hall Sixty Years After," 11. 103-04.

3. For an estimate of the ideals of Bentham's philosophy, see John Stuart Mill, *Utilitarianism, Liberty, and Representative Government* (London, 1910).

4. For a discussion of the anti-Romantic aspects of Utilitarianism, see Jerome Hamilton Buckley, *The Victorian Temper: A Study in Literary Culture* (Cambridge, Massachusetts, 1951), p. 35.

5. John Stuart Mill, *Autobiography* (New York, 1873), pp. 64-65.

6. John Stuart Mill, *Three Essays on Religion* (London, 1885), p. 46.

7. *Ibid.*, p. 62.

8. For a discussion of the changes of Mill's attitude to Benthamism, see Sir Leslie Stephen, *The English Utilitarians* (London, 1950).

9. Compare James Seth, *English Philosophers and Schools of Philosophy* (London, 1912), pp. 284-97.

10. Leonard Huxley, ed., *Life and Letters of Thomas Henry Huxley* (New York, 1932), pp.196-203.

11. See Clarence Ayres, *Huxley* (New York, 1932). Mr. Ayres's estimate of the position of Huxley in the Victorian era is extremely enlightening in view of the advances in modern scientific techniques.

12. Compare John Stuart Mill, *The Positive Philosophy of Auguste Comte* (Boston, 1866). Compare also Basil Willey, *Nineteenth Century Studies* (London, 1949). Willey's chapter on Positivism is one of the shortest and most enlightening estimates of Comte available to the modern reader.

13. Compare Buckley, pp. 5-6, 193-94.

14. See Sir Leslie Stephen, *George Eliot* (New York, 1902) pp. 42-44, 199-200.

15. Again compare Willey's *Nineteenth Century Studies* for a discussion of Positivism and its influence in England.

16. John Henry Newman, *Apologia Pro Vita Sua* (London, 1864), p. 259.

17. For an interesting though narrow Roman Catholic appraisal of Newman's belief, see J. D. Folghera, O. P., *Newman's Apologetic* (London, 1928).

18. "Stanzas from the Grande Chartreuse," 11. 85-86.

19. The best discussion of Arnold's beliefs as expressed in *Culture and Anarchy* is in Lionel Trilling, *Matthew Arnold* (New York, 1938), pp. 252-90.

20. For an interesting analysis of Macaulay's opinions on these ideas, see R. C. Beatty, *Lord Macaulay, Victorian Liberal* (Norman, Oklahoma, 1938).

21. *Past and Present,* chap. II.

22. Two informative studies of Carlyle are Frederick Roe, *The Social Philosophy of Carlyle and Ruskin* (New York, 1921); Hill Shine, *Carlyle and the Saint-Simonians: The Concept of Historical Periodicity* (Baltimore, 1941).

23. Robert Browning, "La Saisaz," *The Complete Poetic and Dramatic Works* (Boston, 1895), p. 854.

24. See D. D. Home, *Incidents in My Life* (New York, 1868), pp. 92ff., 164.

25. Thomas J. Wise, ed. *Letters of Robert Browning* (New Haven, Connecticut, 1933), pp. 78, 115, 116.

26. See Home, pp. 213ff. Compare Edgar Johnson, *Charles Dickens: His Tragedy and Triumph* (New York, 1951) II, 541-42.

27. E. E. Fournier d'Albe, *The Life of Sir William Crookes* (London, 1923), pp. 174-75.

28. Compare Ernest Baker, *The History of the English Novel* (London, 1929), chaps. VIII and IX.

29. Thomas Wright, *The Life of Charles Dickens* (London, 1935), p. 227.

30. For an interesting discussion of the water motif in *Hard Times,* see Buckley, p. 100.

31. See William R. Rutland, *Thomas Hardy: A Study of His Writings and their Backgrounds* (London, 1938), pp. 93ff.

32. Thomas Hardy, "There Seemed a Strangeness," *Collected Poems* (New York, 1937), p. 689. See also "The Darkling Thrush."

33. W. B. Yeats, "The Song of the Happy Shepherd," *Collected Poems* (New York, 1938), p. 7.

34. W. B. Yeats, *Discoveries, Collected Works* (Stratford, 1908), VIII, 47-48.

35. Vera Brittain, *Testament of Youth* (New York, 1938), pp. 198-99.

36. *Ibid.*, p. 199.

37. Shaw Desmond, *The Edwardian Story* (London, 1949), p. 127. See also André Maurois, *The Edwardian Era*, trans. Hamish Miles (New York, 1933). Maurois is, perhaps, a more reliable critic of the period than Desmond, but they are in fundamental agreement concerning the place of Belloc and Chesterton in the history of literature.

38. May Sinclair, *A Defence of Idealism: Some Questions and Conclusions* (New York, 1917), pp. v-vi.

39. Maurois, p. 287.

40. George Bernard Shaw, *Back to Methuselah: A Metabiological Pentateuch* (London, 1949), p. xvi.

41. C. Day Lewis, *A Hope for Poetry* (Oxford, 1945), p. 18.

42. T. S. Eliot, *Collected Poems: 1909-1935* (London, 1936), p. 88.

43. Compare Buckley for a discussion of the "pattern of conversion" in the late Victorian period. Buckley's analysis is interesting in the light that it throws on Eliot's use of the water symbolism.

44. Reference has already been made to the idealistic spirit of the first quarter of the century, as represented in the works of Chesterton and Belloc and, particularly, in Shaw. In my analysis, I merely wish to emphasize the concern with the dangers of materialism.

45. Eliot, "Burnt Norton," *Collected Poems: 1909-1935*, pp. 190-91.

46. Evelyn Waugh, *Brideshead Revisited* (Uniform Edition, London, 1949), pp. 76-77.

47. Graham Greene, "François Mauriac," *The Lost Childhood* (London, 1951), p. 69. Subsequent references are to this edition.

48. Bernard Blackstone, *Virginia Woolf: A Commentary* (London, 1949), p. 69.

49. See Lionel Trilling, *E. M. Forster* (Norfolk, 1943), pp. 113-15.

50. See William York Tindall, *D. H. Lawrence and Susan His Cow* (New York, 1939), pp. 173-74.

51. T. S. Eliot, *After Strange Gods* (London, 1934), p. 54.

52. *Ibid.*, p. 54.

53. *Ibid.*, p. 59.

54. *Ibid.*, p. 60.

55. William York Tindall, *Forces in Modern British Literature: 1885-1946* (New York, 1947), p. 122.

56. *Ibid.*, p. 186.

57. André Gide, *The Journals of André Gide*, trans. Justin O'Brien (New York, 1949), III: 1928-1939, 126. The last paragraph quoted above is particularly interesting in view of Waugh's attitude to the Catholic aristocracy in England. Compare Theresa Marchmain in *Brideshead Revisited.*

58. *Ibid.*, III, 259.

59. *Ibid.*, III, 226.

60. Tindall, pp. 186 ff.

61. Elizabeth Bowen, Graham Greene, and V. S. Pritchett, *Why Do I Write?* (London, 1948), pp. 29-30. Subsequent references are to this edition.

62. *Ibid.*, p. 48.

63. *Ibid.*, p. 49.

64. *Ibid.*, p. 49.

65. Rex Warner, "Freedom in Literary and Artistic Creation," in *Freedom and Culture* (New York, 1951), pp. 210-11.

Chapter Two

1. Kathleen Knott, *The Emperor's Clothes* (London, 1954), pp. 310-11.

2. *Ibid.*, p. 309.

3. Jacques Maritain, *Art and Scholasticism* (New York, 1949), p. 171.

4. *Why Do I Write?*, pp. 31-32.

5. "Henry James: The Religious Aspect," in *The Lost Childhood* (London, 1952), p. 39.

6. *In Search of a Character* (New York, 1961), p. 60. Subsequent references are to this edition.

7. "Henry James: The Religious Aspect," p. 39.

8. François Mauriac, *God and Mammon* (London, 1946), p. 59. Subsequent references are to this edition.

9. "The Lost Childhood," in *The Lost Childhood*, p. 16.

10. *Ibid.*, pp. 15-16.

11. *Ibid.*, p. 17.

12. *The Lawless Roads* (London, 1939), pp. 11-12. Subsequent references are to this edition.

13. "The Revolver in the Corner Cupboard," in *The Lost Childhood*, p. 174.

Chapter Three

1. Evelyn Waugh, "Felix Culpa?" *The Commonweal*, XLVIII (July 16, 1948), 323.
2. "Henry James: The Private Universe," in *The Lost Childhood*, p. 24.
3. "Henry James: The Religious Aspect," in *The Lost Childhood*, p. 39.
4. *A Gun for Sale*, p. 171. References are to the Uniform Edition.
5. The term "anti-hero" is difficult to define. An anti-hero is one who does not measure up to the traditional concept of the heroic figure in an adventure tale or novel. Indeed, the anti-hero appears frequently a villain, Conrad's Kurtz and his Nostromo suggest heroes of different calibers. Greene's Raven and his Pinkie are protagonists, heroes, too. But they are not "heroic" in the accepted sense of the word.
6. Kenneth Allott and Miriam Farris, *The Art of Graham Greene* (London, 1951), p. 110. Subsequent references are to this edition.
7. *The Confidential Agent*. (New York, 1952), p. 58. Subsequent references are to this edition.
8. *The Ministry of Fear*, p. 16. References are to the Uniform Edition.
9. *The Third Man* (New York, 1950), p. 8.
10. "What the Thunder Said," *The Waste Land*, 11. 359-65. Eliot says in a note to *The Waste Land* that the passage was stimulated by ". . . the account of one of the Antarctic expeditions: . . . it was related that the party of explorers, at the extremity of their strength, had the constant delusion that there was *one more member* than could actually be counted."
11. *Our Man In Havana* (New York, 1958), p. 7. Subsequent references are to this edition. One is reminded of the villain "Carter" in "The Lost Childhood."

Chapter Four

1. *It's a Battlefield*, p. 218. References are to the Uniform Edition.
2. "The Other Side of the Border," in *Nineteen Stories* (New York, 1949), p. 211.
3. *England Made Me*, p. 11. References are to the Uniform Edition.
4. Francis Kunkel, *The Labyrinthine Ways of Graham Greene* (New York, 1959), pp. 43-56. Kunkel astutely points out aspects of Pinkie Brown's character that derive from Minty.

Chapter Five

1. Sean O'Casey, *Rose and Crown* (New York, 1952), p. 272.
2. *Brighton Rock*, p. 9. References are to the Uniform Edition.

3. "The Young Dickens," in *The Lost Childhood,* p. 56.

4. *The Lawless Roads,* p. 160.

5. "Frederick Rolfe: Edwardian Inferno," in *The Lost Childhood,* p. 93.

6. *The Power and the Glory,* pp. 10-11. References are to the Uniform Edition.

7. The rose is, of course, a reference to Dante's multifoliate rose and to the rose in Eliot's "Ash Wednesday."

8. Evelyn Waugh, "Felix Culpa?" *The Commonweal,* XLVIII (July 16, 1948), 324.

9. *Why Do I Write?,* p. 32. One is reminded of James's urgent plea to a friend that he not finish an anecdote, for in it James found the germ of a story; foreknowledge of the ending might have encouraged him to influence the actions of the characters.

10. Allott and Farris, p. 214.

11. In *The Labyrinthine Ways of Graham Greene,* Francis Kunkel says, "I contend that *The Heart of the Matter* would be a truer, finer, and more forceful picture of life if Greene had made more of Scobie's neurotic attitude towards suffering and his neurotic sympathy for the plight of women and children and less use of jumbled theology." This sort of reasoning seems futile to me, for the novel stands as Greene has written it.

12. *The Heart of the Matter,* p. 141. References are to the Uniform Edition.

13. Martin C. D'Arcy, "The Anatomy of a Hero," *Transformation Three,* eds. Stefan Schimanski and Henry Treece (London, n.d.), pp. 16-18.

14. The reader is, of course, reminded of Mauriac's *The Desert of Love.*

15. "François Mauriac," in *The Lost Childhood,* p. 69.

16. *Ibid.,* p. 70.

17. *Ibid.,* p. 71.

18. Evelyn Waugh, "The Heart's Own Reasons," *The Commonweal,* LIV (August 17, 1951), 458.

19. Georges Bernanos, *The Diary of a Country Priest,* trans. Pamela Morris (New York, 1937), pp. 123-24.

20. Norman Shrapnel, Review of *The End of the Affair,* the *Manchester Guardian,* September 7, 1951, p. 4.

21. *The End of the Affair* (New York, 1951), p. 21. Subsequent references are to this edition.

22. Compare Paul Rostenne, *Graham Greene: témoin des temps tragiques* (Paris, 1949), pp. 218 ff. Also for a discussion of Greene's use of Existentialist philosophy, compare Robert Evans, "Existentialism

in Graham Greene's *The Quiet American,*" *Modern Fiction Studies,* 111 (Autumn 1957), 241-48.

23. *The Quiet American* (New York, 1956), p. 32. Subsequent references are to this edition.

24. *In Search of a Character,* p. xiii.

25. *A Burnt-Out Case* (New York, 1961), p. 16. Subsequent references are to this edition.

26. Orville Prescott, "Books of the Times," *The New York Times,* February 17, 1961, p. 25.

27. *Ibid.*

Chapter Six

1. *The Living Room,* Intro. by Peter Glenville (London, 1957), p. ix.

2. *The Living Room* (London, 1953), p. 58. Subsequent references are to this edition.

3. "The Second Death," in *Nineteen Stories,* p. 157.

4. *Ibid.*

5. *The Potting Shed* (London, 1957-58), p. 69. Subsequent references are to this edition.

6. *The Complaisant Lover* (London, 1959), p. 69. Subsequent references are to this edition.

Chapter Seven

1. *God and Mammon,* p. 37.

2. *Great Men,* trans. Elsie Pell (London, 1952), p. 117.

3. *Journey Without Maps,* Uniform Edition, p. 10.

4. *In Search of a Character,* p. 31.

5. "Henry James: The Private Universe," in *The Lost Childhood,* p. 30.

6. "François Mauriac," in *The Lost Childhood,* pp. 69-74.

7. *God and Mammon,* p. 52.

Chapter Eight

1. Claire Eliane Engel, *Esquisses anglaises: Charles Morgan, Graham Greene, T. S. Eliot* (Paris, 1949), p. 69.

2. Evelyn Waugh, "Felix Culpa?" *The Commonweal,* XLVIII (July 16, 1948), 324.

3. Walter Allen, "The Novels of Graham Greene," *Penguin New Writing,* XVIII, 148-60. Subsequent references to Allen are to this essay.

4. George Woodcock, *The Writer and Politics* (London, 1948), pp. 151-52.

5. Arthur Calder-Marshall, "Graham Greene," *Living Writers,* ed. Gilbert Phelps (London, 1947), pp. 39-47.

6. Kenneth Allott and Miriam Farris, *The Art of Graham Greene,* pp. 24-25.

7. Paul Rostenne, *Graham Greene: témoin des temps tragiques,* p. 218. The discussion of Greene as a novelist is very hazy. Rostenne prefers to use Greene as a stalking horse so that he may move into all sorts of philosophical and literary discussions pertinent to the modern French novel. The discussion of Greene is weak since Rostenne prefers to neglect the English backgrounds and to talk about Greene vaguely in connection with Bernanos, Sartre, and Céline. Rostenne's reading is wide, but he fails to appreciate the force of Roman Catholicism as an important factor in what he calls "la vision Greenienne." His explanation of Existentialism, especially when it is relative to Roman Catholicism, seems very tenuous. The discussion by Marcel Gabriel in H. J. Blackman, ed. *Six Existentialist Thinkers* (London, 1952), pp. 66-85, is much more illuminating.

8. Robert J. North, *Le Catholicisme dans l'oeuvre de François Mauriac,* Intro. Gaétan Bernoville (no publisher, 1950), pp. xxii-xxvi.

9. Jacques Madaule, *Graham Greene* (Paris, 1949), p. 368.

10. John Atkins, *Graham Greene* (London, 1957).

11. Francis Kunkel, *The Labyrinthine Ways of Graham Greene.*

12. *Time,* October 29, 1951, p. 103.

Selected Bibliography

I am indebted to Professor Maurice Beebe, editor of Modern Fiction
Studies, *for his permission to use the bibliography and checklist of*
Graham Greene studies published in Modern Fiction Studies, III (Au-
tumn 1957), 269-88. *For a nearly complete bibliography published*
since this study, see Graham Greene: Some Critical Considerations, *ed.*
R. O. Evans (Lexington, Kentucky, 1963).

There are many editions of Greene's works available; and what I
have done below is to list chronologically and as exactly as possible
the facts of original publication. Greene's work has been assembled,
but not fully, into a Uniform Edition *by William Heinemann, Ltd.,*
and I have indicated these dates in square brackets for the benefit of
the reader. I have also listed those books and articles about Greene
that I feel the interested reader would find most useful in the section
entitled Secondary Sources.

GREENE'S WORKS

1. Major Works

Babbling April. Collected poems. Oxford: Basil Blackwell, 1925.
The Man Within. London: Heinemann, 1929. [Uniform Edition, 1952.]
The Name of Action. London: Heinemann, 1930. [Withdrawn.]
Rumour at Nightfall. London: Heinemann, 1931. [Withdrawn.]
Stamboul Train; an entertainment. London: Heinemann, 1932. Pub-
    lished in the United States under the title of *Orient Express* (Gar-
    den City: Doubleday, 1932). [Uniform Edition, 1947.]
It's a Battlefield. London: Heinemann, 1934. [Uniform Edition, 1948.]
The Basement Room. London: Cresset Press, 1935. Includes: The Base-
    ment Room; Brother; A Chance for Mr. Lever; A Day Saved;
    The End of the Party; I Spy; Jubilee; The Lottery Ticket; The
    Other Side of the Border (unfinished novel); Proof Positive.
England Made Me. London: Heinemann, 1935. Published in the
    United States as *The Shipwrecked* (New York: Viking, 1953).
    [Uniform Edition, 1947.]

Journey Without Maps; A Travel Book. London: Heinemann, 1936.
[Uniform Edition, 1950.]

A Gun for Sale; an entertainment. London: Heinemann, 1936. Published in the United States under the title of *This Gun for Hire*
(Garden City: Doubleday, 1936). [Uniform Edition, 1947.]

Brighton Rock. London: Heinemann, 1938. [Uniform Edition, 1947.]

The Confidential Agent; an entertainment. London: Heinemann, 1939.
[Uniform Edition, 1952.]

The Lawless Roads. London: Longmans, 1939. Published in the United
States under the title *Another Mexico* (New York: Viking, 1939).

The Power and the Glory. London: Heinemann, 1940. Published in
the United States as *The Labyrinthine Ways* (New York: Viking,
1940), and reissued in 1946 under the original English title.
[Uniform Edition, 1949.]

The Ministry of Fear; an entertainment. London: Heinemann, 1943.
[Uniform Edition, 1950.]

Nineteen Stories. London: Heinemann, 1947. Contains the stories published in *The Basement Room and Other Stories,* listed above,
plus the following: Across the Bridge; Alas, Poor Maling; The
Case for the Defense; A Drive in the Country; The Innocent; A
Little Place Off the Edgeware Road; Men at Work; The Second
Death; When Greek Meets Greek.

The Heart of the Matter. London: Heinemann, 1948. [Uniform Edition, 1951.]

The Third Man; an entertainment. New York: Viking, 1950. Published
as a story in *American Magazine,* CXLVII (March 1949), 142-
60.

The Fallen Idol; an entertainment. In *The Third Man and The Fallen
Idol.* London: Heinemann, 1950. A retelling of "The Basement
Room."

The Lost Childhood and Other Essays. London: Eyre and Spottiswoode, 1951. Contains the following essays:
At Home; Beatrix Potter; Bombing Manoeuvre; Book Market;
Burden of Childhood; Dr. Oates of Salamanca; Domestic Background; Don in Mexico; Eric Gill; Fielding and Sterne; Film
Lunch; Ford Madox Ford; Francis Parkman; François Mauriac;
Frederick Rolfe: Edwardian Inferno; From Feathers to Iron;
George Darley; Great Dog of Weimar; Harkaway's Oxford; Henry
James: The Private Universe; Henry James: The Religious Aspect; Herbert Read; Hoax on Mr. Hulton; Invincible Ignorance;
Isis Idol; Last Buchan; Lesson of the Master; Lost Childhood;
Man Made Angry; Mr. Cook's Century; Plays of Henry James;
Poker-face; Portrait of a Lady; Portrait of a Maiden Lady; Remembering Mr. Jones; Revolver in the Corner Cupboard; Samuel

Butler; Saratoga Trunk; Ugly Act; Unheroic Dramatist; Unknown War; Vive le Roi, Walter de la Mare's Short Stories; Young Dickens.

The End of the Affair. London: Heinemann, 1951. [Uniform Edition, 1955.]

The Living Room; a play in two acts. London: Heinemann, 1953.

Twenty-One Stories. London: Heinemann, 1954, Uniform Edition. Contains the same stories published in *Nineteen Stories,* listed above, substituting for The Lottery Ticket and The Other Side of the Border the following: The Blue Film; The Destructors; The Hint of an Explanation; Special Duties.

Loser Takes All; an entertainment. London: Heinemann, 1955.

The Quiet American. London: Heinemann, 1955.

The Potting Shed; a play in three acts. London: Heinemann, 1957-58.

Our Man in Havana; an entertainment. London: Heinemann, 1958.

The Complaisant Lover; a comedy. London: Heinemann, 1959.

A Burnt-Out Case. London: Heinemann, 1961.

In Search of a Character: Two African Journals. London: The Bodley Head, 1961.

A Sense of Reality. London: The Bodley Head, 1963. Contains the following stories: Under the Garden; A Visit to Morin; Dream of a Strange Land; A Discovery in the Woods.

2. Other Stories by Graham Greene

"The Bear Fell Free." London: Grayson and Grayson, 1935. [Grayson Books.]

"Beauty." *Esquire,* LIX (April 1963), 60, 142.

"Church Militant." *The Commonweal,* LXII (January 6, 1956), 350-52.

"Dream of a Strange Land." *The Saturday Evening Post,* January 19, 1963, pp. 44-47.

"The Escapist." *Spectator,* CLXII (January 13, 1939), 48-49.

"The Lieutenant Died Last." *Colliers,* CV (June 29, 1940), 9-10.

"Mortmain." *Playboy,* March, 1963, pp. 77, 110 ff.

"News in English." In *Alfred Hitchcock's Fireside Book of Suspense,* ed. Alfred Hitchcock (New York: Simon and Schuster, 1947).

"Voyage in the Dark." *Spectator,* CLXI (September 16, 1938), 437.

3. Children's Books

The Little Fire Engine. London: Parrish, 1950. Published in the United States as *The Little Red Fire Engine.* New York: Lothrop, Lee and Shepard, 1952.

The Little Horse Bus. London: Parrish, 1952.

The Little Steam Roller. New York: Lothrop, Lee and Shepard, 1955.

4. Non-Fiction

The Best of Saki. Selected and with an introduction, "The Burden of Childhood," by Graham Greene. London: British Publisher's Guild, 1950.
British Dramatists. London: W. Collins, 1942 ["Britain in Pictures" series.]
The Old School, Essays by Divers Hands. Edited and with an introduction and essay, "The Last Word," by Graham Greene. London: Jonathan Cape, 1934.
Why Do I Write? An exchange of views between Elizabeth Bowen, Graham Greene, and V. S. Pritchett. London: Percival Marshall, 1948.

5. Essays and Articles

"Analysis of a Journey." *Spectator,* CLV (September 27, 1935), 459-60.
"Before the Attack." *Spectator,* CXCII (April 16, 1954), 456.
"The Blind Eye." *Spectator,* CLXI (July 1, 1938), 13.
"Boatload of Politicians." *Spectator,* CLV (December 6, 1935), 938-39.
"Books in General." *New Statesman and Nation.* XXXIV (October 11, 1947), 292; XXXVIII (Augut 20, 1949), 198; XXXIX (January 28, 1950), 101; XLII (July 14, 1951), 45; XLIII (June 21, 1952), 745; XLVI (July 18, 1953), 76; XLVIII (October 2, 1954), 411.
"The Catholic Church's New Dogma: Assumption of Mary." *Life,* XXIX (October 30, 1950), 50-52ff.
"The Catholic Temper in Poland." *Atlantic Monthly,* CXCVII (March 1956), 39-41.
"La civilisation chrétienne est-elle en peril?" *La Table Ronde,* No. 2 (1948), 211-23.
"Convoy to West Africa." In *The Mint, Volume I,* ed. Geoffrey Grigson (London: Routledge, 1946), pp. 40-55.
"The Dark Backward: A Footnote." *London Mercury,* XXXII (October 1935), 562-65.
"A Day at the General's." *Spectator,* CLX (April 15, 1938), 670. Also published as "A Day with Cedillo," *q.v.*
"A Day with Cedillo." *Living Age,* CCCLIV (June 1938), 330-32. Also published as "A Day at the General's." *q.v.*
"Dear Mr. Chaplin." *New Republic,* CXXVI (October 13, 1952), 5. Also published as "The Return of Charlie Chaplin: An Open Letter."
"Death in the Cotswolds." *Spectator,* CL (February 24, 1933), 247.

Selected Bibliography

"Devil Blacksmith." *Spectator*, CLVI (March 6, 1936), 393-94.
"Dictator of Grand Bassa." *Spectator*, CLVI (January 17, 1936), 89-90.
"Diem's Critics." *America*, XCIII (May 28, 1955), 225.
"The Entertainments of A. E. W. Mason." *New Statesman and Nation*, XLIV (October 4, 1952), 381.
"H. Sylvester." *The Commonweal*, XXXIII (October 25, 1949), 11-13.
"Ideas in the Cinema." *Spectator*, CLIX (November 19, 1937), 894-95.
"Indo-China." *New Republic*, CXXX (April 5, 1954), 13-15.
"Indochina Journal." *The Commonweal*, LX (May 21, 1954), 170-72.
"Last Act in Indo-China." *New Republic*, CXXXII (May 9, 1955), 9-11; (May 16, 1955), 10-12.
"London Diary." *New Statesman and Nation*, XLIV (November 22, 1952), 593.
"Malaya, the Forgotten War." *Life*, XXXI (July 30, 1951), 51-54ff.
————. Abridged in *Reader's Digest*, LIX (November 1951), 119-23.
"Message aux catholiques français." *Dieu Vivant*, No. 14 (1949), 31-35.
"Middle-brow Film." *Fortnightly*, CXLV (n. s. CXXXIX) (March 1936), 302-07.
"New Reels." *Spectator*, CLXIII (September 29, 1939), 443.
"Norman Douglas." *Spectator*, CLXXXVIII (March 14, 1952), 332.
"Oslo and Stockholm." *Living Age*, CCCXLV (January 1934), 424-26.
"Les paradoxes de christianisme." *Dieu Vivant*, No. 18 (1951), 35-42.
"The Pope Who Remains a Priest." *Life*, XXXI (September 24, 1951), 146-48ff.
"Revenge." *The Commonweal*, LXI (January 14, 1955), 403-04.
"Selection of Film Criticisms." Reprinted from *Spectator*. In *Garbo and the Night Watchman*, ed. Alistair Cooke (London: Jonathan Cape, 1937), pp. 208-39.
"Self-Portrait." *Spectator*, CLXVII (July 18, 1941), 66ff.
"Strike in Paris." *Spectator*, CLII (February 16, 1934), 229-30.
"Subjects and Stories." *In Footnotes to the Film*, ed. Charles Davey (London: Lovat Dickson, 1937).
"Three Score Miles and Ten." *Spectator*, CLXVI (February 14, 1941), 171.
"To Hope Till Hope Creates." *New Republic*, CXXX (April 12, 1954), 11-13.
"Twenty-four Hours to Metroland." *New Statesman and Nation*, XVI (August 13, 1938), 250.
"Two Capitals." *Spectator*, CLI (October 20, 1933), 520-21.

SECONDARY SOURCES

Albères, R. M. "Graham Greene et résponsibilités." In his *Les hommes traqués*. Paris: La Nouvelle Editions, 1953, pp. 157-85. Discusses the problem of the individual's responsibility to a religious ethic.

Allen, Walter, "Graham Greene." Denys Val Baker, ed. *Writers of To-day*. London: Sidgwick, 1946, pp. 15-28. (Previously published as "The Novels of Graham Greene." *Penguin New Writing*, XVIII (1943), 148-60.) Discusses philosophy of Greene's novels in terms of Augustinism and Pelagianism.

———. "Awareness of Evil: Graham Greene." *Nation*, CLXXXII (April 21, 1957), 344-46.

Allen, W. Gore. "Evelyn Waugh and Graham Greene." *Irish Monthly*, LXXVII (January 1949), 16-22. A comparison of the two writers' approach to Catholicism. Says the driving impulse of Greene's world is evil; not so, Waugh's.

Allott, Kenneth, and Miriam Farris. *The Art of Graham Greene*. London: Hamish Hamilton, 1951. Sees Greene's work in terms of obsessions such as "the divided mind," and "the fallen world."

Atkins, John. *Graham Greene: A Biographical and Literary Study*. New York: Roy Publishers, 1958. Studies themes and relates early novels and characters to later works. Includes biographical information.

Beebe, Maurice. "Criticism of Graham Greene: A Selected Checklist with an Index to Studies of Separate Works." *Modern Fiction Studies*, III (Autumn 1957), 281-88.

Bernoville, Gaétan. "Introduction." *Le Catholicisme dans l'oeuvre de François Mauriac*, by Robert J. North. Paris: Editions du Conquistador, 1950. Says that Greene makes his fable pleasing by utilizing the figure of the pathetic Christian.

Birmingham, William. "Graham Greene Criticism: A Bibliographical Study." *Thought*, XXVII (Spring 1952), 72-100.

Bouscaren, Anthony T. "France and Graham Greene versus America and Diem." *Catholic World*, CLXXXI (September 1955), 414-17. Discusses French attitude toward Catholicism.

Boyle, Alexander. "Graham Greene." *Irish Monthly*, LXXVII (November 1949), 519-25. Discusses Greene's Catholic point of view.

———. "The Symbolism of Graham Greene." *Irish Monthly*, LXXX (1952), 98-102. Discusses Greene's use of traditional and private symbols.

Braybrooke, Neville. "Graham Greene." *Envoy*, III (September 1950), 10-23.

———. "Graham Greene, a Pioneer Novelist." *College English*, XII (October 1950), 1-9. A good discussion of themes in *Brighton Rock* and *The Heart of the Matter*.

———. "Graham Greene as Critic." *The Commonweal*, LIV (July 6, 1951), 312-14.

Selected Bibliography

Buckler, William E., and Arnold B. Sklare. *Stories from Six Authors.* New York: McGraw-Hill, 1960. General introduction to the art of Greene for the student.

Calder-Marshall, Arthur. "Graham Greene." Gilbert Phelps, ed. *Living Writers: Being Critical Studies Broadcast in the B. B. C. Third Programme.* London: *Sylvan Press,* 1947. Says Greene's chief concern as a novelist is social.

Codey, Regina. "Notes on Graham Greene's Dramatic Technique." *Approach,* No. 17 (1955?), 23-27. Discusses Greene's use of religiously oriented subject matter.

Connolly, Francis X. "Inside Modern Man: The Spiritual Adventures of Graham Greene." *Renascence,* I (Spring 1949), 16-24. Discusses Greene's concern with Roman Catholicism.

Costello, Donald P. "Greene and the Catholic Press." *Renascence,* XII (Autumn 1959), 3-28. Discusses Greene's reception by the contemporary Catholic press.

Cottrell, Beekman W. "Second Time Charm: The Theatre of Graham Greene." *Modern Fiction Studies,* III (Autumn 1957), 249-55. Discusses Greene's handling of religious themes in his dramas.

DeVitis, A. A. "Allegory in *Brighton Rock." Modern Fiction Studies,* III (Autumn 1957), 216-25. Explanation of form of *Brighton Rock.*

————. "The Church and Major Scobie." *Renascence,* X (Spring 1958), 115-20. Considers Scobie as modern tragic hero.

————. "The Entertaining Mr. Greene." *Renascence,* XIV (Autumn 1961), 8-24. Looks at themes and characters in the Entertainments.

Ellis, William D., Jr. "The Grand Theme of Graham Greene." *Southwest Review,* XLI (Summer 1956), 239-50. Discusses the problem of Greene's heroes and their sense of sin.

Engel, Claire Eliane. *Esquisses anglaises: Charles Morgan, Graham Greene, T. S. Eliot.* Paris: Editions Je Sers, 1949. Sees Greene's work as tinged with Jansenism; the Calvinist ethic becomes a dominant motif.

Evans, R. O., ed. *Graham Greene: Some Critical Considerations.* Lexington, Kentucky: University of Kentucky Press, 1963.

————. "Existentialism in Graham Greene's *The Quiet American" Modern Fiction Studies,* III (Autumn 1957), 241-48. Sees the novel as conforming to certain aspects of Sartrian Existentialism.

Findlater, Richard. "Graham Greene as Dramatist." *Twentieth Century,* CLVI (June 1953), 471-73. Looks at Greene's use of the stage as vehicle for his themes.

Gardiner, Harold C. "Graham Greene, Catholic Shocker." *Renascence,*

I (Spring 1949), 12-15. Discusses the disquieting effect of Greene's work on many readers.

Gregor, Ian. "The New Romanticism: A Comment on *The Living Room.*" *Blackfriars,* (September 1953), 403-06. Good discussion of characterization.

Grubbs, Henry A. "Albert Camus and Graham Greene." *Modern Language Quarterly,* X (March 1949), 33-42. A view of Greene against Existentialist philosophy.

Haber, Herbert R. "The Two Worlds of Graham Greene." *Modern Fiction Studies,* III (Autumn 1957), 256-68. The two worlds are the world of the spirit and the world of men.

Hargreaves, Phyllis. "Graham Greene: A Selected Bibliography." *Bulletin of Bibliography,* XXII (January-April 1957), 45-48. Reprinted with additions, *Modern Fiction Studies,* III (Autumn 1957), 269-80.

Herling, Gustav. "Two Sanctities: Greene and Camus." *Adam,* No. 201 (1950), 10-19. The problem of existentialist background is looked at critically.

Hoggart, Richard. "The Force of Caricature· Aspects of the Art of Graham Greene, with Particular Reference to *The Power and the Glory.*" *Essays in Criticism,* III (October 1953), 447-62.

Jerrold, Douglas. "Graham Greene, Pleasure-Hater." *Harper's,* CCV (August 1952), 50-52. Calls Greene "the finest living novelist, bar one, in our language."

Karl, Frederick R. *The Contemporary English Novel.* New York: Farrar, Straus and Cudahy, 1962. Looks at Scobie as tragic hero.

Kunkel, Francis L. *The Labyrinthine Ways of Graham Greene.* New York: Sheed and Ward, 1960. An examination of Greene's maturing artistry.

Lewis, R. W. B. "The Fiction of Graham Greene: Between the Horror and the Glory." *Kenyon Review,* XIX (Winter 1957), 56-75. Considers the plan of *The Power and the Glory.*

———. "Graham Greene: The Religious Affair," in *The Picaresque Saint: Representative Figures in Contemporary Fiction.* New York: Lippincott, 1959.

———. "The 'Trilogy' of Graham Greene." *Modern Fiction Studies,* III (Autumn 1957), 195-215. Considers the themes that lend unity to the three novels published between 1938 and 1948.

McCarthy, Mary. "Graham Greene and the Intelligentsia." *Partisan Review,* XI (Spring 1944), 228-30. Discusses Greene's appeal as a popular writer.

Madaule, Jacques. *Graham Greene.* Paris: Editions du Temps Présent, 1949. Says one of Greene's chief problems as a writer is the Protestant audience for which he writes; that Green has a horror of the optimism that Protestantism has developed in the Anglo-Saxon world.

Marshall, Bruce, "Graham Greene and Evelyn Waugh." *The Commonweal*, LI (March 3, 1950), 551-53. Points out obvious points of difference in approach to religion.

Mesnet, Marie-Beatrice. *Graham Greene and the Heart of the Matter*. London: Cresset Press, 1954. Looks at the major novels and comments on characterization, themes, and techniques.

Newby, P. H. *The Novel, 1945-1950*. London: Longmans, 1951. Places Greene in a literary perspective.

O'Donnell, Donat. "Graham Greene: The Anatomy of Pity." In his *Maria Cross: Imaginative Patterns in a Group of Modern Catholic Writers*. New York: Oxford University Press, 1952. Sees Greene from a rather narrow point of view; discusses the problem of grace.

O'Faolain, Sean. "Graham Greene: I Suffer; Therefore, I Am." In his *The Vanishing Hero: Studies in Novelists of the Twenties*. London: Eyre and Spottiswoode, 1956.

————. "The Novels of Graham Greene: *The Heart of the Matter*." *Britain Today*, No. 148 (August 1948), 32-36. Discussion of Scobie's role in the novel.

Osterman, Robert. "Interview with Graham Greene." *Catholic World*, CLXX (February 1950), 356-61.

Pange, Victor de. *Graham Greene*. Préface de François Mauriac, et un texte inédit de Graham Greene traduit par Marcelle Sibon. Paris: Editions Universitaires, 1953. Excellent discussion of the role of the lieutenant in *The Power and the Glory*.

Patten, Karl. "The Structure of *The Power and the Glory*." *Modern Fiction Studies*. III (Autumn 1957), 225-34. Looks at the novel in terms of symbolical identifications and spatial patterns.

Prescott, Orville. "Comrade of the Coterie." In his *In My Opinion*. Indianapolis: Bobbs-Merrill, 1952, pp. 92-109. Discusses Greene's Roman Catholic orientation.

Pritchett, V. S. "The World of Graham Greene." *New Statesman* (January 4, 1958), pp. 17-18. Discussion of Greene's unhappy world.

"Propos de table avec Graham Greene." *Dieu Vivant*, No. 16 (1950), 127-37. Transcript of conversation between Greene and several French critics.

Reed, Henry. *The Novel Since 1939*. London: Longmans, 1947, pp. 15-18. Places Greene in literary perspective.

Rewak, William J., S. J. "*The Potting Shed*: Maturation of Graham Greene's Vision." *Catholic World* CLXXXVI (December 1957), 210-13. Comments on action and structure and Greene's thematic material.

Rischik, Josef. *Graham Greene und Sein Werk.* Bern: Verlag A. Francke Ag., 1951. Discusses Greene's predilection for the "seedy," the unhappy, and the disoriented.

Rostenne, Paul. *Graham Greene: témoin des temps tragiques.* Paris: Juillard, 1949. Discusses the novels as possible Existentialist exemplifications.

Roy, Jean-H. "L'Oeuvre de Graham Greene ou un christianisme de la damnation." *Les Temps Modernes,* LII (1950), 1513-19.

"Shocker." *Time,* LVIII (October 29, 1951), 98-104. (Anonymous profile.) Brief résumé of Greene's career to publication of *The End of the Affair.*

Shuttleworth, Martin and Simon Raven. "The Art of Fiction III: Graham Greene." *Paris Review,* I (Autumn 1953), 24-41. (Interview.) Questions posed to Greene concerning the craft, philosophy, and theory of the artist.

Traversi, Derek. "Graham Greene." *Twentieth Century,* CXLIX (1951), 231-40, 319-28. Discusses themes in *Brighton Rock* and in *The Heart of the Matter.*

Turnell, Martin. "The Religious Novel." *The Commonweal,* LV (October 26, 1951), 55-57. Discusses Greene's Catholicism as rationale for the novels.

Voorhees, Richard, "Recent Greene," *South Atlantic Quarterly,* LXII (Spring 1963), 244-55. Comments on later fiction; says Greene's later work is compelling because of the dilemma by which it is plagued.

————. "The World of Graham Greene." *South Atlantic Quarterly,* L (July 1951), 389-98. Says Greene's combination of naturalistic description and Christian sense of sin makes him a moralist as well as a novelist.

Wansbrough, John. "Graham Greene: The Detective in the Wasteland." *Harvard Advocate,* CXXXVI (December 1952), 11-13, 29-31. Discusses technique.

Wassmer, Thomas A. "The Problem and Mystery of Sin in the Works of Graham Greene." *The Christian Scholar,* XLIII:4 (Winter 1960), 309-15. Examines Greene's use of Roman Catholic themes.

Waugh, Evelyn. "Felix Culpa?" *The Commonweal,* XLVIII (July 16, 1948), 322-25. Discusses Scobie's suicide and Roman Catholic implications.

West, Anthony, "Graham Greene." In his *Principles and Persuasions.* New York: Harcourt Brace, 1957.

Woodcock, George. "Graham Greene." In his *The Writer and Politics.* London: Porcupine Press, 1948, pp. 125-53. Discusses Greene and Communism.

Wyndham, Francis. *Graham Greene.* Bibliographical Series of Supple-

Selected Bibliography

ments to *British Book News on Writers and Their Work,* No. 67. London: Longmans, 1955.

Zabel, Morton Dauwen. "Graham Greene: The Best and the Worst." In his *Craft and Character in Modern Fiction.* New York: Viking, 1957. (Earlier versions of this essay were included in *Forms of Modern Fiction,* edited by William Van O'Connor (Minneapolis: University of Minnesota Press, 1948), pp. 287-93; in *Critiques and Essays on Modern Fiction 1920-1951,* edited by John W. Aldridge (New York: Ronald Press Company, 1952), pp. 518-25; and in *Der Monat* (Berlin), in 1953.) One of the best treatments of Greene that has been written.

Index

Index